OUR CONTEXT

Exploring Our Congregation and Community

Mark D. Johns

Augsburg Fortress

Minneapolis

OUR CONTEXT
Exploring Our Congregation and Community

Developed in cooperation with the Division for Congregational Ministries of the Evangelical Lutheran Church in America, Michael R. Rothaar, project manager.

A portion of chapter 9 is adapted from *Developing Effective Committees*, by Michael R. Rothaar, copyright © 1993, Augsburg Fortress.

Scripture quotations are from New Revised Standard Version Bible, copyright © 1989 Division of Christian Education of the National Council of the Churches of Christ in the United States of America. Used by permission.

Series overview: David P. Mayer, Michael R. Rothaar
Editors: Laurie J. Hanson, Andrea Lee Schieber, James Satter

Cover design and series logo: Marti Naughton
Text design: James Satter
Cover photograph: Gordon Gray, FRPS

About the cover image: The centerpiece of the Resurrection Window in First Lisburn Presbyterian Church, Northern Ireland, was created by stained glass artist James Watson, Belfast, from fragments of church windows destroyed by a car bomb in 1981 and restored after a second bomb in 1989. The window symbolizes new life in Christ, which transforms darkness to light, hatred to love, despair to hope, and death to life. The members of First Lisburn Presbyterian have lived out this promise through new initiatives for community service, reconciliation, and peace-making.

ISBN 978-0-8066-4404-2

The paper used in this publication meets the minimum requirements of American National Standard for Information Sciences—Permanence of Paper for Printed Library Materials, ANSI Z329.48-1984.

Contents

Series Overview

Welcome to the Congregational Leader Series, and welcome to the journey of discovering God's future for you and your congregation. Your congregation's mission and ministry are given to you by God. We sometimes refer to "our church," but it is always Christ's church. We are at best its stewards or caretakers, not its owners. As we plan, organize, and lead, we strive toward excellence in everything we do to reflect the glory and grace of God, who has entered human life to redeem us.

As a congregational leader, you may be asking, "What is our mission? How should we structure things? How can we plan for the future and where will the resources come from?" The Congregational Leader Series provides resources for effective planning and leadership development. Each book includes biblical and theological foundations for planning and leadership development, and practical information to use in building on your congregation's strengths.

We are first of all called to be faithful to God's word and will. Exploring the Bible enables us to discern what God's plan is for us as individuals and as a congregation. Ignoring or minimizing the centrality of God in our deliberations risks not only failure but also our faith. In the words of the psalmist, "Unless the LORD builds the house, those who build it labor in vain"(Psalm 127:1).

Why should we engage in congregational planning and leadership development? When the congregation is at its best, these activities aid us in fulfilling our mission to the world: reaching out with the gospel of Jesus Christ. Faithful planning for mission mirrors God's activity in the world, from creating and covenant-making to gathering and renewing the church. When congregations fail to plan, they risk dissipating the resources they have been given by God and begin falling away from all that God has intended for them.

In short, faithful planning and leadership development engage the congregation and all its members in the creative work of God. Continually analyzing and shaping our vision, mission, ministry, and context allows us to ask, "What is God calling our congregation to be?" Working to develop and support leaders enables us to ask, "How has God gifted each of us for ministry?"

We begin with prayer

As congregational leaders, we always begin our endeavors with prayer. Discerning God's will for us is a task that requires that we be in communication with God. Unfortunately, we often come up with new ideas and programs—and then pray that God will bless them! That order needs to be reversed. Our prayers should precede our plans, helping us discern God's call to us.

In his few years of public ministry, Jesus accomplished a tremendous amount of healing, teaching, and service for others. However, his ministry did not begin until after he had spent an extended period of time in the wilderness reflecting on his call and God's purpose for his life. Following that retreat, virtually every moment of his life's story was punctuated with prayer and ultimately concluded with his supplications in Gethsemane and on the cross.

Paul wrote to the Thessalonians, "Rejoice always, pray without ceasing, give thanks in all circumstances; for this is the will of God in Christ Jesus for you" (1 Thessalonians 5:16-18). These words were meant for us—congregational leaders anxious to get on with things that need to be done. Notice how Paul places *prayer* between *rejoice* and *thanks* in this verse. Prayer is not simply another task to be done nor an obligation to be met. It is a gift of God to be celebrated and used with joy and thanksgiving. It is meant to permeate our lives. As leaders, we are seeking to construct God's will in our communities. God invites us to build with gladness and to make prayer the mortar between every brick we lay.

As congregational leaders, we always begin our endeavors with prayer.

We build from strength

Most leadership resources begin with the assumption that there is a problem to be solved. In the midst of the real problems that surround us, however, our task as congregational leaders is to identify the strengths, giftedness, and blessings that God has given to us and the congregation. Our primary calling is not to be problem-solvers but to be asset-builders. Paul reminds us, "Let all things be done for building up"(1 Corinthians 14:26). This is not license to ignore problems, conflicts, or deficiencies. Rather, it is a call to view the brokenness around us in a new way.

Our role as Christian leaders is to attempt to look at our congregation, our fellow Christians, and ourselves, as God sees us. "This is my commandment, that you love one another as I have loved you" (John 15:12). Jesus did not blindly ignore the problems around him. Instead, he viewed those problems through a lens of love, appreciation, and forgiveness. We are called to build from strength, to construct our plans and visions from what God has given us. When we try to build from weakness and focus only on our problems, we compound both and ultimately fail.

> **Our primary calling is not to be problem-solvers but to be asset-builders.**

First Church was located in a growing, well-to-do suburb, on a main thoroughfare, and in a beautiful new building. The members of First Church appeared to have everything going for them, and the congregation's future looked very bright.

The congregation, however, faced an ongoing problem with mortgage payments. This problem became so all-consuming that the congregation began to lose sight of its strengths, gifts, and mission for the future. The members of First Church had everything they needed to solve the problem of mortgage payments but they were unable to stop fixating on it. Soon, many other issues surfaced as everyone became a fault-finder.

Today there is no mortgage-payment problem because there is no First Church. The preoccupation with weakness and deficiency blinded the congregation to the reality of its gifts. This congregation died, not because of its problems but because of its perspective.

We must constantly ask ourselves and others, "Where is God at work here? What gifts have we received for ministry in this place?" Focusing only on what we don't have breeds jealousy, competition, hopelessness, and lost vision. Focusing on our gifts gives birth to joy, affirmation, and hope.

We won't find quick fixes

We live in a culture obsessed with quick fixes and mesmerized by the notion that there is a prescription for every ailment and accident. But things keep falling apart. People get sick. Programs fail. Committees don't function. Plans backfire. And goals aren't met. The list of mistakes, failures, misfires, and flops grows and grows. In his letter to the Romans, Paul reminds us that "all have sinned and fall short of the glory of God"(Romans 3:23). Paul says this not to weigh us down with despair, but instead to remind us that our salvation comes from God and not ourselves.

Faithful leaders have a deep respect for the reality of problems and obstacles. Things will always fall apart. That's why planning, assessing, goal-setting, leading, and visioning are ongoing processes, not quick fixes. As leaders, we need to know the nature of sin and publicly acknowledge its pervasiveness. Then we can lead, not with unhealthy fatalism, but with honesty, humility, and a sense of humor.

We are all ministers

As Christians, everything we do and plan is communal. We cannot plan unilaterally or devise strategies in isolation. To be sure, each of us has received salvation individually through baptism, but at that moment, through the water and the Word, we were united with the body of Christ. Even the gifts that God has given each of us are meant for the common good of all God's people: "To each is given the manifestation of the Spirit for the common good" (1 Corinthians 12:7).

In other words, each of us is a minister, whether pastor or lay person, and each of us is called to serve others. This is a radical departure from our culture's overwhelming emphasis on individual

Each of us is a minister, whether pastor or lay person, and each of us is called to serve others.

independence. The idea that we are all ministers and that as the church we minister as a community has tremendous implications for all of our planning and development efforts.

Leadership development is nothing more than equipping the members of the congregation so that they are strengthened for ministry: "The gifts he gave were that some would be apostles, some prophets, some evangelists, some pastors and teachers, to equip the saints for the work of ministry, for building up the body of Christ" (Ephesians 4:11-12). Paul would be appalled at the idea that a paid professional minister should carry out all of the ministry of the congregation or that only some people in the congregation are called to ministry.

Faithful planning and leadership development affirm that all of God's people are gifted and invited to participate in ministry. Identifying, embracing, and strengthening each other's gifts for common mission is a daunting task that never ends, but through that effort and in that journey we become what God intended: "But you are a chosen race, a royal priesthood, a holy nation, God's own people, in order that you may proclaim the mighty acts of him who called you out of darkness into his marvelous light" (1 Peter 2:9).

A model for understanding congregations

Congregations are extremely complex. Throughout the Congregational Leader Series, we invite you to look at your congregation through a particular model or set of lenses. This model helps us to understand why congregations are so complex, and it provides some important clues for the leadership skills and tasks that are needed.

A congregation resembles three different institutions at the same time: a *community of spiritual formation*, a *voluntary association*, and a *nonprofit organization*. This isn't a matter of size—the largest and smallest are alike in this. It isn't a matter of context—the model applies to both urban and rural settings. Each type of institution has different values and goals, which may even contradict each other. Each of these values and goals requires different things from leaders.

Communities of spiritual formation

A congregation is, in part, a community of spiritual formation. People come to such a community to join with others in growing closer to God. They seek to understand God's word and God's will for their life. They seek an experience of God's presence, a spiritual or emotional awareness of transcendence and love. They seek time for contemplation and prayer, and also time to work with others on tasks that extend God's love to others.

How are our congregations communities of spiritual formation? Much of congregational life centers on worship. We teach children and adults the practice of faith. The church provides support in Christ's name during times of crisis and need. We engage in visible and public activities, such as offering assistance to people who are homeless, or hungry, or survivors of abuse, as a way of both serving God and proclaiming God's mercy and justice.

The most important value in a community of spiritual formation is authenticity. There is no room for pretense, no room for manipulation, and no room for power games. The goals we establish must be clearly directed to outcomes in people's spiritual lives. The fundamental question for self-evaluation is this: "How has our ministry brought people closer to God?"

The most important value in a community of spiritual formation is authenticity.

Voluntary associations

Like any club or voluntary association, a congregation is a gathering of people who are similar to one another in specific ways, share a common purpose, and largely govern and finance their organization's existence and activities. In addition, people often find that belonging to a club is a way to make friends and social or business contacts, and enjoy meaningful leisure time activities. Some voluntary associations, such as Kiwanis or Lions clubs, have charitable purposes and sometimes seek support from people beyond their own membership. Some voluntary associations are focused on common interests or activities, such as gardening or providing youth athletic leagues.

Membership requirements may be strict or fluid, costs may be high or low, and commitments may be long or short, but they are spelled out rather clearly. A number of unwritten rules may serve to get people to conform to common values. Most voluntary associations would like to have more members, both to strengthen their organization and to expand the social benefits that come from a broader circle. But the new members usually are people who are very much like those who are already members.

The most important value in a voluntary association is effectiveness in helping people relate to one another.

The most important value in a voluntary association is effectiveness in helping people relate to one another. The goals are largely relational. There must be many opportunities for people to form relationships, especially with those with whom they have much in common. The association must operate in such a way that people all feel that their own values and hopes are being well served, usually through direct access to the decision-making process and ample opportunities for public dissent. People want and expect to be contacted regularly by both leaders and other members, and to feel that they are fully accepted as part of the group.

It is also important that there is a consensus—a shared vision—on what the association is and does. When conflict emerges, it must be negotiated and resolved. Because membership is voluntary, when there's conflict, or when they just don't feel part of the group anymore, people are usually quick to withhold their financial support or quit altogether.

Nonprofit organizations

As if it weren't complicated enough to be both a community of spiritual formation and a voluntary association, now consider that your congregation is also a nonprofit organization. It is a chartered or incorporated institution, recognized as a legal entity by the federal, state, and municipal government. A congregation can borrow and lend, sue and be sued. You as a congregation are accountable to society and responsible for following all applicable laws. Almost all congregations are property owners and employers. The congregation has formal operational procedures and documents (from your constitution to state laws) that dictate how you must make decisions and conduct your affairs. The usually unspoken but fundamental goal of a nonprofit organization is self-perpetuation, making sure that the institution will continue.

In this regard, congregations are similar to any business that offers services to the public. Being *nonprofit* simply means that the organization's assets can't be distributed to individuals or for purposes contrary to the charter. It doesn't mean that the congregation can't or shouldn't be run in a businesslike manner—or that it can't accumulate assets. The actual operation doesn't differ much from that of a profit-making business. In a nonprofit organization, the primary value is efficiency, or achieving the greatest results with the least possible expenditure of resources.

Another core value is continuity, with orderly systems that must be applied by anyone who carries out the organization's work. To reach financial goals, a nonprofit organization seeks voluntary contributions and often regularizes revenue through endowments and ancillary sources of income. Efforts are made to minimize costs without sacrificing quality. The organization also tries to build reserves to meet unanticipated circumstances and periodic needs (such as replacement of depreciating assets). Policies are in place to protect the staff and volunteers, and to ensure clear and mutually agreed upon expectations. There are clear lines of accountability and each person operates within a specified scope of decision-making.

Planning in a nonprofit organization includes making the best use of property and facilities. The property is seldom an end in itself, but the goal of leadership is always to maximize its usefulness. Other organizational goals revolve around having a truly public presence, including marketing effectively, identifying the needs and wants of a particular group of people, developing a product or service that addresses those needs, and informing the target group of its desirability and availability. Nonprofit organizations must do this as surely and skillfully as those in the profit sector.

In a nonprofit organization, the primary value is efficiency, or achieving the greatest results with the least possible expenditure of resources.

You may have heard that "you shouldn't be a manager, you should be a leader." This is unfortunate language, because management is part of leadership, and voluntary organizations need managers. How you analyze, organize, delegate, supervise, and evaluate the congregation's work is critical to its vitality.

Leadership

What does the word *leadership* really mean? Think of it as having three dimensions: *character*, *knowledge*, and *action*. *Character* permeates all three aspects of this model. Leaders have principles and try to live them out. In any of the three ways in which we're looking at congregations, leaders are honest, trustworthy, dedicated, caring, disciplined, and faithful to the core principles—and have many more virtues as well. Although everyone sins and fails, be clear that improvement is expected from all leaders.

It is not only character that counts. Leaders must also know things and do things. *Knowledge* and *action* can be developed. They can be learned in books and classes or from working with people who have expertise. Things we know from one part of our experience can be applied to other parts of our lives.

Applying the congregational model

The three-part model of congregations is helpful in exploring the different things that leaders must be, know, and do in a community of spiritual formation, in a voluntary association, and in a nonprofit organization.

Problems develop when the values, goals, and leadership styles appropriate to one part of the congregational model are mistakenly applied to one of the others. It is not wrong to value authentic spirituality, effective interpersonal relationships, and operational efficiency. There are times when each of these should be given the highest priority. Recognize that your congregation probably has emphasized one of these areas at the expense of the others, and plan your way to a better balance. Embrace the wonderful complexity of congregational life and ask God to move among us to change us and renew us and rededicate us to God's own purposes.

The Congregational Leader Series

This is one of several books in the Congregational Leader Series. The entire series seeks to build on the positive, basing your planning on assets rather than deficiencies, and to focus on outcomes, enabling your congregation to make a specific and definable difference in people's lives. The series has two sets: congregational planning and leadership development. Books in this series can be used in any order, so you can get started with those books that are most helpful for you and your congregation. The reproducible tools can be used with your council, committees, planning teams, leadership groups, and other members of the congregation. Visit www.augsburgfortress.org/CLS to download and customize these tools.

Faithful planning and leadership development take us on a journey, a pilgrimage, and an exploration of God's possibilities for you and your congregation. The Congregational Leader Series provides resources for your travels, as you seek God's will and guidance for you and your congregation.

This image of a cross indicates that further information on a topic appears in another book in the Congregational Leader Series.

Chapter 1

Tools of the Trade

For we are God's servants, working together; you are God's field, God's building. According to the grace of God given to me, like a skilled master builder I laid a foundation, and someone else is building on it. Each builder must choose with care how to build on it. For no one can lay any foundation other than the one that has been laid; that foundation is Jesus Christ.

—1 Corinthians 3:9-11

Congratulations!

By picking up this book you have shown that you want your congregation to better carry out its mission of proclaiming the gospel. Perhaps your congregation faces some particular crisis or difficulty at the moment, or perhaps it's just time for a fresh start or a new phase. In any case, you have some exciting challenges ahead. And whether it is through changing outward circumstances or through that small voice within, the Holy Spirit is calling your congregation and its leaders to examine what and where you are, and to wrestle with where you might go and what you might become. The fact that you are seeking a book such as this indicates that you are looking for ways to understand what is happening and to contribute to positive outcomes.

What can this book do for us?

This book will help you and other congregational leaders to examine, understand, and cope positively with changes. This book is a tool. But just as no carpenter can set her tools next to a pile of lumber and expect to come back to find a finished house, simply reading this book will do very little. This book offers some general insights about congregations but, more importantly, it offers questions to be raised and discussed among a variety of congregational members and leaders. The tools in the back of the book offer information and exercises that you can use with groups in your congregation to better understand your own particular context.

This book is a guide to a process of self-examination. The process itself may be as valuable as the information that you collect from it, because the process will help congregational leaders to communicate to one another about the heritage they treasure, the assumptions they make about the present, and the visions they have for the future. Discussing the questions at the end of each chapter will help your congregation focus on its mission in ways that will involve a widening circle of congregational members.

This book is a guide to a process of self-examination.

GIGO

Before examining this process further, here is a brief word of caution: As congregations face changes, there often is pressure to find a quick fix that will solve all problems overnight. There are even books on the market that promise just such a quick fix. You will not find any all-encompassing promises here, however. Only people inspired with the gospel and empowered by the Spirit can bring about positive congregational change. This book will offer some ways to ignite and channel that energy, but it is not a package of "Instant Holy Spirit."

Computer programmers have coined the term GIGO, an acronym that stands for "Garbage In, Garbage Out." Programmers know that no matter how powerful the machine or how well-written the software, if the information entered into the system is sloppy or incorrect the resulting output will be meaningless.

The same is true as congregations begin the process of understanding themselves, their circumstances, and their mission. If the input into the process is based on the same old assumptions, the likely output will point toward doing the same old things the same old way, whether those things work or not. GIGO. So, this book will accomplish for you and your congregation only what you make of it. If you're ready to really look at what God is calling you to be as a congregation, ready to follow where Christ is leading you, then this will be an exciting endeavor.

When would such a process be helpful?

There are a variety of situations that may cause a congregation and its leaders to want to take stock of the congregation's present circumstances and future plans. Sometimes congregations find themselves in times of rapid growth, which place a strain on facilities and bring newcomers unfamiliar with congregational procedures and traditions. Alternatively, congregations sometimes find themselves in periods of declining membership that cause concerns about vitality, resources, or even the congregation's future survival. Congregations may also need to take stock whenever they enter a new chapter in their history that may open the door to new ministry opportunities. Such times of transition may occur when a congregation calls a new pastor or other leadership staff member, pays off a debt, receives a bequest, completes a new or additional facility, or experiences (or contemplates) any other significant change in its circumstances.

At such times of change and transition, a congregation must first identify and challenge old assumptions. When things have changed all around, one cannot simply proceed as if no changes had occurred. Yet often congregations are slow to recognize and adjust to change. There's a cliché that "the seven last words of the church" will be "We've never done it that way before." Such a saying may be humorous, but it reflects the truth that organizations tend to resist change until forced to recognize the need for it. A thorough examination of a congregation and the community it serves can assist congregational leaders and members to recognize the new situation in which they find themselves and to adapt to it more quickly and painlessly than waiting for a crisis to thrust the congregation toward change.

A congregation in north central Iowa assumed that its members were basically a cross section of the community and that the congregation represented the town as a whole. Farmers, business people, and laborers seemed to be among the people in the pew.

After a process of self-examination and considering the community it serves, the congregation discovered that while its membership may have been a fair representation of the town several decades ago, in more recent years a large number of schoolteachers, physicians, and white-collar business people had been attracted to the church. Many neighbors actually described their congregation as "the church for people who had been to college." This image was actually scaring away some people who might have become members of the congregation. Old assumptions kept this congregation from seeing itself as its neighbors saw it, and only by examining itself and its community could those old assumptions be changed.

Congregational leaders sometimes do sense the changing winds that blow around them and react instinctively. However, leaders should confirm their hunches or suspicions before committing resources to significant new ministries or launching major changes in congregational structures. A process of self-examination can aid leaders in verifying what they already suspect to be true, and assist them in interpreting their ideas to the congregation as a whole. While some congregations may trust their leaders enough to approve a major new expenditure because the pastor "just has a feeling" it will be good, most members will want clear indications of needs, trends, and goals before they are convinced. A process of self-examination can provide objective data for interpretation and communication.

A process of self-examination can provide objective data for interpretation and communication.

Healthy organizations engage in periodic planning updates or "pulse taking." Just as individuals go to the doctor periodically for a check up—even when they are feeling well—healthy congregations examine themselves and their surroundings from time to time to see if there are potential problems that can be caught before they become crises, or to consider opportunities that were previously unseen.

While preparing for its centennial celebration, a Midwestern congregation found that the articles of incorporation on file with the state and county governments specified "the disciplines of the Church of Denmark," rather than the congregation's current constitution and bylaws, as the binding code for resolving disagreements or holding elections in the congregation. This might have made sense 100 years ago, but if the congregation had recently become involved in legal matters, such as a lawsuit or large insurance claim, such a document would have caused great confusion.

Every congregation will want to take a look in the mirror from time to time.

Similarly, congregations sometimes discover that their governing documents are out of date and in need of an overhaul. When an overhaul of legal documents, constitutions, or bylaws is called for, it's a good idea to engage in a process of self-evaluation to make sure that new documents reflect current practices and procedures clearly and accurately.

Certainly, every congregation will want to undertake a serious self-study in anticipation of changes in leadership. When a pastor leaves after a number of years of service, it is vital that the congregation carefully take stock of where it has been, where it is going, and what strengths and leadership qualities the next pastor will need to lead in that direction.

In summary, congregations should look forward to taking a thorough look at themselves and their surroundings whenever they anticipate changes of any kind—whether good or bad—and periodically in-between times of major change, just to avoid being surprised. The old adage that "nothing stays the same except change" fits well with congregations that are vital and alive. Every congregation will want to take a look in the mirror from time to time.

What does such a process involve?

A self-examination begins by looking outward, with an inventory of what sorts of people currently make up the community which is the context for the congregation's ministry. A fresh look at the community can reveal fresh opportunities for outreach and ministry. The congregation then considers what it might do to take advantage of these opportunities—what gifts are available and in what ways it might organize itself anew for mission. The final step in the process involves building support among congregational members and seeing to the necessary details of setting a new organization for ministry in place. The chapters of this book will guide you through these steps. Other resources in the Congregational Leader Series will assist in this process.

Who should participate in this process?

In a thorough physical examination, the doctor looks the patient over from head to toe. So it is with a congregational self-examination. To be really thorough, every part of the congregation needs to be involved.

A small group of congregational leaders will need to steer the self-examination process. The size of this group will vary, depending on a number of factors, but generally, a group of six to eight people will be about right. If fewer than six people attempt to steer the process, it will be difficult to accomplish all necessary tasks in a timely fashion and represent the full scope of congregational concerns. A group larger than 12, on the other hand, will not function as a small group and will become formal in conversation. So the steering group should be no smaller than six and no larger than 12 in number, although it will be better to keep the group size in the smaller end of this range. The rest of this chapter will provide some ideas about who might be included, to help trigger your thinking about the important constituent groups and key leaders in your congregation.

Staff

Certainly any paid or volunteer congregational staff will have a stake in the outcome of a serious congregation self-study, because the process and its results could point to significant changes in the way they carry out their duties and new priorities for the way staff time is used. Even more, your pastor and any other staff members provide a living storehouse of information about the current day-to-day operations of the congregation's ministries.

In most congregations, the pastor is both the primary spiritual leader and the key administrative leader. Unless this self-study is taking place because the pastor has left or is about to leave, the pastor will need to play a major role in any process of self-examination and should be part of the group conducting the self-examination process. In congregations served by more than one pastor, it is important that each pastor provide input to the process. One or two pastors should serve on the steering group itself.

Today, even very small congregations may have a fairly large number of lay staff. These may include a secretary, custodian, musicians, preschool or day-care directors, volunteer coordinators, Associates in Ministry, diaconal ministers, and so forth. Some may be full-time employees, but most will be part-time staff or volunteers. All are immensely important to the congregation's ministries and will have vital input for the process of self-examination. But unless a particular staff member's role in the congregation is especially central, such as a full time Associate in Ministry serving a congregation together with one pastor, it will be difficult to include one staff member without including all as part of the steering group.

Council

The congregation's council is its board of directors and highest decision-making body unless the entire voting membership of the congregation is convened. The members of the council will all be very important to the self-examination process. In some cases, it may make sense to simply have the council become the steering group. In any case, the council should be represented on the steering group, perhaps by the council chairperson or president, or by several members or officers of the council.

Committees, boards, teams, and task groups

Most congregations distribute ministry tasks among a variety of groups with responsibilities for specific areas of concern, such as worship, education, stewardship, finance, and evangelism. Because the process of self-examination will look closely at such groups and how they function, each of the existing groups will be important to the process. There will probably be too many of these groups to incorporate a representative from each in the steering group. However, steering-group members need to be familiar with the congregation's structure and how ministry groups have functioned in the past.

Many congregations have a small group that advises the pastor, such as a ministry partnership or mutual ministry committee. Such committees are often small, chosen to be representative of the entire congregation, and accustomed to openly discussing the big picture of congregational ministries. Such a group may be very well suited to steering the process of self-examination.

Auxiliary groups

Most congregations also have a number of groups organized to provide ministries to and with certain segments of the congregation's members. These may include youth groups, women's groups (such as Women of the ELCA), men's groups, and organizations for seniors. Again, it is probably impossible for each of these to be represented in the steering group, but the steering group will better voice the concerns of the whole congregation if it is diverse. Whatever other qualifications they may have, make sure that the members of the steering group represent a cross section of the congregation's membership. Include people of different ages. There should be about equal numbers of men and women. If the congregation is fortunate enough to have diversity in terms of ethnic backgrounds, this diversity should be represented. Although the steering group will not legislate or make decisions for the congregation's future, it will certainly need to listen to the widest possible spectrum of voices.

Make sure that the members of the steering group represent a cross section of the congregation's membership.

Informal structures

In many congregations there are informal structures: family con-
nections, relationships in the local business community, factions
remaining from past disagreements in the congregation, or other
alignments or well defined groups. Part of the process of self-examination will involve bringing such informal structures to light and
determining where they fit into the congregation's ministry. At this
point, however, if such structures are evident, it will be best to recognize them, though perhaps not on the steering group.

Different roles in the play

Listing all of the various key leaders, task or mission groups,
elected or appointed bodies, auxiliaries, constituencies, and informal
structures in your congregation is a first step toward self-evaluation.
These people and groups represent the roles being played and the
relationships through which your congregation's ministry and community life are carried out. Selecting six or eight people who know
and can represent these roles and relationships as they steer the self-
examination process sets things in motion. But each of the people and
groups you've listed will play a part in this process.

Unless the entire congregation knows something about the process,
and has some input into it, any results or suggestions for future
objectives and strategies that grow from the process will likely be

A pastor serving a small parish in the Southwest observed that more than one-third of the members of the congregation were members of the same extended family. The undisputed head of this family was a widow in her 80s simply known as "Grandma." The pastor noted that although she served in no elected congregational office, no major decision in the congregation could be made until Grandma had been consulted and her approval was assured.

challenged. At a minimum, the congregation council should bless the process by officially appointing the steering group. Possibly the selection could be ratified by a vote at a congregational meeting. The pastor can help the steering group's work to be recognized by conducting an installation ceremony at a worship service.

Ask the editors of bulletins and newsletters to include news of the planning process so that all congregational members are aware that a process of prayerful reflection is underway. This process will take time, and over the weeks and months the steering group will want to report its progress regularly to the council and congregation through whatever means are available. Open lines of communication are essential. From time to time, the steering group will approach various committees, groups, auxiliaries, or key people, requesting information, opinions, or feedback. The communication channels will work in both directions.

Above all, assure the congregation that the process of self-examination is not a threat, but an opportunity—for that is what it truly is. It is an opportunity for the congregation to listen more closely to God's call, discerning its unique direction and mission. And it is an opportunity to discover or rediscover the congregation's gifts and resources for making ministry more effective, vital, and dynamic.

Congratulations! Just by considering the possibilities, thinking through the list of significant individuals and groups, and by contemplating the opportunities before you, you have already done a great deal. The tools are in your hands and the process has already begun.

Assure the congregation that the process of self-examination is not a threat, but an opportunity.

Continuing the conversation

As emphasized in the series overview at the beginning of this book, prayer is an essential part of seeking God's will for your congregation. As you gather to consider your first steps in this process, join in prayer with those who have gathered with you to discuss your congregation's future. Pray that you may be open to the Spirit's leading. Pray that God will bless your efforts. Pray that your eyes may be

opened to see beyond old assumptions, and that your minds may be
open to new ideas. And finally, thank God for the abundant gifts that
have sustained your congregation through its history, and which will
continue to enrich its future.

Questions for discussion

1. What particular changes, challenges, or opportunities does your
   congregation face that lead you to consider entering into a process
   of self-examination?

2. How would you describe your congregation to a stranger? What are
   the most significant or unique ministries in which your congregation is currently engaged, and why does your congregation choose
   to focus on these areas?

3. Who are the key leaders of this congregation? What is it about these
   people that causes other congregational members to look up to
   them and to follow their leadership?

4. Make a list of the various committees, boards, task groups, auxiliaries, or other relationships that exist in your congregation. What
   are the responsibilities and expectations of each? Who are the key
   leaders of each?

5. What is working particularly well in your congregation's organizational structure today? What committees, boards, or task groups
   are the strongest and most creative in their work? Which are
   struggling?

6. List the half dozen most committed, energetic, and capable members of your congregation who might be able to lead the congregation in an objective and open minded examination of itself.

7. As you see it, what is the Holy Spirit calling your congregation to
   be and to do right now and in the foreseeable future?

Chapter 2

Biblical and Confessional Foundations

I believe that by my own understanding or strength I cannot believe in Jesus Christ my Lord or come to him, but instead the Holy Spirit has called me through the gospel, enlightened me with his gifts, made me holy and kept me in the true faith, just as he calls, gathers, enlightens, and makes holy the whole Christian church on earth and keeps it with Jesus Christ in the one common, true faith. Daily in the Christian church the Holy Spirit abundantly forgives all sins—mine and those of all believers. On the Last Day the Holy Spirit will raise me and all the dead and will give to me and all believers in Christ eternal life. This is most certainly true.

—Explanation to the Third Article of the Creed
in Martin Luther's Small Catechism,
Robert Kolb and Timothy J. Wengert, eds., *The Book of Concord*
(Minneapolis: Augsburg Fortress, 2000), pp. 355-356

What does the Bible say about congregations?

Scripture is the final authority for whatever a congregation does. Indeed, the *Model Constitution of the Evangelical Lutheran Church in America* states, "This congregation accepts the canonical Scriptures of the Old and New Testaments as the inspired Word of God and the authoritative source and norm of its proclamation, faith, and life" (Provision C2.03. Evangelical Lutheran Church in America, 2001). But the Bible does not provide a single model of what a congregation should look like, how it should be organized, or what its specific tasks should be. Rather, Scripture provides a number of different models that have been used by people of faith in different times, places, and

For more
discussion on
congregational
organization, see
*Our Structure:
Carrying Out
the Vision.*

circumstances. Several of these models are explored in the first part of this chapter and in the Leadership Bible Study on pages 99-103.

The clear message that is conveyed by the wide variety of structural models in the Bible is that congregations organize themselves in various ways depending on their circumstances. Each model has particular attributes that help make congregations successful in certain social contexts and types of situations. Under the guidance and direction of the Holy Spirit—and in keeping with its denominational traditions—a congregation is free to organize itself in whatever way suits its particular context. In studying a variety of models, it is possible to learn important concepts about how a congregation might be organized in your particular situation. In this way, even though the Bible does not provide a single model, it will nevertheless be the "authoritative source and norm" for your congregation's faith and life.

Judges versus kings

See "A Leadership
Bible Study" on
pages 99-103.

One of the oldest models of leadership and organization in the Bible can be found in the book of Judges. At that time, a *judge* was a charismatic leader who answered the call to act at a time when the nation, their tribe, or their village faced an immediate crisis—usually an enemy attack.

The system of leadership by judges had advantages, but it also had serious disadvantages. While there were no ongoing responsibilities or burdens in maintaining governmental structures during times of peace and tranquility, a lot of people had to suffer before a crisis was recognized, a judge emerged, and an adequate response could be organized. The people of Israel eventually noticed that neighboring tribes that had united into nation states with strong, centralized permanent governments responded to threats much more quickly.

The last of the judges was Samuel, the devout priest and fiery prophet who led Israel through a series of crises—some military (brought about by the attacks of the Philistines) and some spiritual (brought about by lapses in faith and morals). During Samuel's lifetime, the people of Israel asked God to give them a king. The king would unite the tribes into one nation, establish a permanent government to anticipate problems, create a trained professional military, and could make decisions quickly in times of crisis.

Samuel warned that, because God alone is truly capable of ruling as king, a human king would inevitably make mistakes, some of which could be very costly. Samuel's prophetic warnings were quickly fulfilled in Israel's first king, Saul—who proved not to be up to the task—and its second, David, who allowed kingly power to bend his personal moral compass. Since then, organizations of all types, including congregations, have had to find a balance between too little authority in leadership and too much.

> **Organizations of all types, including congregations, have had to find a balance between too little authority in leadership and too much.**

The temple model

Israel's third king, Solomon, finally fulfilled his father's ambition to build a splendid temple as a dwelling place for God among the people. Solomon's temple—and the temple of Herod, which was built to replace it after the first had been destroyed by invaders—were both operated by the Levites, the descendants of Moses' brother, Aaron. Only the Levites were permitted to offer sacrifices, perform other rituals, and enter the innermost sanctuaries of the temple. The Levites did it all, and those who came to the temple to offer their sacrifices were primarily spectators, watching the priest perform.

Although there may still be Levites in some congregations, most pastors usually prefer that members take an active, rather than passive, role. But some members may have become comfortable as spectators. When Levites are suddenly absent, for whatever reason, a congregation may have difficulty adjusting.

The apostolic model

The book of Acts includes an idyllic account of life in the very first Christian congregation in Jerusalem. We may wonder if such an ideal congregation ever really existed. We know for certain that it didn't last very long, as conflicts soon emerged. At first the apostles tried to act

Conflict and disagreement are normal in congregations.

like priests, doing everything. This soon failed, and a new system emerged. While the key policy decisions were based on faith precepts without worrying about business concerns, the mechanics of putting those policies into practice was very pragmatic. The apostles were devoted to preaching and teaching, while deacons took care of the congregation's day to day needs. No spectators here! Everyone had a role to play.

Paul's letters

Clearly, the book of Acts is not the only place in the New Testament that describes congregations in conflict. In fact, almost every one of Paul's letters or epistles is written in response to some sort of crisis taking place in a congregation. In some instances these situations were relatively practical and personal—such as when Paul addressed Philemon on the matter of how to deal with an escaped slave, or when Timothy was given advice on church administration. In other instances the epistles were addressed to congregations struggling with the most fundamental issues of the faith—such as when the Thessalonians wrestled with questions concerning Christ's second coming, or the Galatians were being lured into false beliefs and practices that cut to the very heart of the gospel.

See *Our Community: Dealing with Conflict in Our Congregation.*

What this indicates very plainly is that conflict and disagreement are normal in congregations. Because Christians are, in Martin Luther's terms, "simultaneously justified yet sinners," human sin remains alive even among the most faithful individuals and the communities in which they live, worship, and serve.

The stories of so many New Testament congregations in conflict, however, also should teach us to be discerning about the conflicts and crises we face. Some disagreements, like those at Galatia and Thessalonica, are indeed about fundamental issues central to the faith. Many more, like those in the letters addressed to Timothy or Philemon, are about matters in which the stakes are much lower, and in which the concerns are practical and pastoral matters.

John's Revelation catalog

In the second and third chapters of Revelation, the last book of the New Testament, the exiled John writes to seven congregations that are under his pastoral care. Even though these congregations were located in the same geographic area, shared a common language, culture, political and economic situation, each was different from the others and was addressed in a unique way.

Likewise, congregations today are unique, no matter how much they may have in common with their neighbors. Because congregations in our society share so much in common, despite their location, size, denominational affiliation, ethnic heritage, or traditions, a similar process can be employed to understand each. Yet because of these and many other unique attributes, there is no "one size fits all" solution to the challenges congregations face. Your congregation is not exactly like the one across the street, across town, or in the next state. The similarities will allow your congregation to learn from its neighbors, but the differences will make it impossible to copy exactly what your neighbors are doing.

The Old and New Testaments do not show a single picture of leadership or organization. Instead, they show that the people of God have organized themselves in a variety of different ways according to the different circumstances in which they were called to live and serve. Sometimes it worked best to be very loosely organized, while other times strong, centralized leadership was required. Sometimes it was important to have a large professional staff in place to carry out most of the ministry, and other times it was much more effective to let professionals do only certain specialized tasks, and to encourage many volunteers to handle a vast array of other necessary tasks.

The people of God have always faced conflicts and crises in their life and work together, and sometimes these conflicts have concerned vitally important, fundamental issues of faith. More often, however, conflicts and crises have surrounded pastoral concerns and different approaches to day to day challenges. And in every instance, we see

The Old and New Testaments do not show a single picture of leadership.

For more on leadership styles, see *Our Gifts: Identifying and Developing Leaders*.

that each community of faith, no matter how similar it may be to others, is also unique in the gifts it has been given for ministry and in the ministry challenges it must face.

Scripture is not the only source of insights about the way congregations live and work. The doctrinal roots of a congregation's faith tradition also speak to its identity, as do the time and place in which it is called to minister. The following section will examine some of the roots shared by Lutheran congregations. If you belong to another denomination, you may find useful parallels here, but you also may wish to consult some of your own confessional documents at this point. Chapter 3 in this book will discuss cultural influences common to all congregations in North America, regardless of faith tradition.

What do the Lutheran confessions say about congregations?

Lutherans have a fixed body of writings that have guided their understanding of the faith and institutional life for nearly 500 years. However, like Scripture, these confessional documents are open to a certain amount of interpretation. As with the Bible, the confessions do not provide one clear picture of the congregation, but several. Over the last five centuries Lutherans have organized their congregations and other church institutions in a wide variety of ways, all of which are consistent with the confessions.

The Lutheran confessions do not always specifically address congregations, but often speak in broader terms about the whole Christian church. The relationship between the wider church and the local congregation will be examined in chapter 4. For the moment, however, it is assumed that most of what the confessions have to say about the larger church will apply directly to the congregation as well.

The Small Catechism

Many Lutherans study a portion of the confessions in Confirmation classes—Martin Luther's Small Catechism. And the part of the Small

Catechism that deals most directly with the church is Luther's explanation to the Third Article of the Apostles' Creed (which appears on page 25).

There are at least three themes running through these words of Luther's that are important for congregations. First, the church is not merely a human institution, but is called into existence by the Holy Spirit. It is the Spirit that calls, gathers, enlightens, and makes holy both the individual members and the entire collective body. Left to human understanding or strength, the church would not exist. Second, the church is always a corporate entity. Individual believers gather together, and those who have been thus gathered are, in turn, kept "with Jesus Christ in the one common, true faith." There is no such thing as an isolated Christian, or an individual congregation—all are kept together. Third, the day-to-day business of the church is the proclamation of the forgiveness of sins and the promise of eternal life.

What is true of the church as a whole is true for each congregation as well. If members do not believe that their congregation was called into existence by God's Spirit, the congregation will lack a sense of identity. If a congregation does not understand itself to be a gathering of people called together—and at the same time gathered, itself, into a larger whole of the church—it will lack a sense of unity. And if a congregation does not keep its primary mission clearly in mind, it will lack purpose.

The Augsburg Confession

Many Lutherans are not as familiar with the Augsburg Confession as with the Catechism. The Augsburg Confession was written in the city of Augsburg, Germany, in the year 1530. The primary author was Martin Luther's close friend and associate, Dr. Philip Melanchthon. The original intent was to present the beliefs of the Lutherans to the leaders of Germany in a way that would help them understand that Lutheran teaching was consistent with the doctrines and practices of the church from ancient times. Although it was rejected by the

> The church is not merely a human institution, but is called into existence by the Holy Spirit.

emperor, in the years following the Augsburg Confession became the defining statement of Lutheran teaching.

Article VII of the Augsburg Confession states: "It is also taught that at all times there must be and remain one holy, Christian church. It is the assembly of all believers among whom the gospel is purely preached and the holy sacraments are administered according to the gospel" (*The Book of Concord*, p. 42).

Congregations are *church* only when they do church.

These words don't sound terribly controversial to us today, but they were earth-shattering in the 16th century. Here, Protestants were defining the church not as a place, such as Rome or the regional cathedral, nor as a person, such as the pope or the bishop. Rather, the church is said to exist as a corporate body—the people among whom the Word of God is preached and the sacraments are administered. The church is not defined by a person or a place, such as a priest standing before a consecrated altar, but rather the place and the people are defined by the act of "doing church." (The writer is indebted to Dr. Timothy J. Wengert, Professor of Reformation History at the Lutheran Theological Seminary at Philadelphia, for the insights shared here concerning the interpretation of Article VII of *The Augsburg Confession*.) The distinction is subtle but extremely important.

In the next chapter we will see that, sociologically, congregations fulfill various social roles and functions, and that congregations exist as complex social institutions. But the Augsburg Confession reminds us that however important these other roles and functions may be, congregations are *church* only when they *do church*. However excited congregations may become about their identity, their sense of community, their heritage, or their success, it is important to remember that, first and foremost, congregations exist to *do church*—to proclaim the word of God's grace and to celebrate grace in water, and in bread and wine. A congregation may be many things to many people, and may do many positive things for its members and its community, but it is only the church when the Word and the sacraments remain central to its identity and mission. Thus, only when the congregation and its leaders keep these things central will all else fall into place.

Continuing the conversation

As you gather with those who are concerned with the process of self-examination, begin as always with prayer. Thank God for the gift of the Bible and the witness of the people of God who have gone before us, and for the variety of circumstances in which God's people have been called to minister, and the variety of forms that ministry has taken. Ask God to more clearly reveal your congregation's circumstances and to help you more clearly discern its gifts. Above all, thank God for the partnership you share with other believers in this congregation, and that which you share with other congregations as you strive to remain faithful to your calling to *do church* in your place.

Questions for discussion

1. Which of the scriptural models most closely resembles your congregation today? Why?

2. Think about conflicts that have recently emerged in your congregation. Were they conflicts about how things should be done or conflicts over matters vital to the Christian faith?

3. What does it mean for your congregation to be a "gathering" of people called by the Holy Spirit? How is the fact that members are "called, gathered, enlightened and made holy" lived out in your congregation's daily life?

4. What does it mean for your congregation to be part of a "gathering" of other congregations that belong to a larger church? How is this expressed in your congregation's daily life?

5. In what ways does your congregation demonstrate that its first priority is *doing church* in Word and sacraments?

Chapter 3

Cultural Foundations

Religious subcultures, or "socio-religious communities" as they have
sometimes been called, function simultaneously as communities, associations, and symbolic orders. People may belong to them in a deep
communal sense or simply associate with them as they would with any
other voluntary organization. They may identify with them symboli-
cally and form moral and religious judgments about them, positively or
negatively. Emotionally they involve attachments with varying degrees
of intensity. Far more than just theology, or doctrine, or institution,
socio-religious communities locate people in social space, defining
them over against religious others.

—Wade Clark Roof, *Spiritual Marketplace:*
Baby Boomers and the Remaking of American Religion

Sociology lessons

Not only do we have the benefit of the Bible and the confessions as
guides to understanding what congregations are all about, but today
we also have the insights of experienced social scientists. These
insights can be extremely helpful in applying the principles of the
Bible and our confessional heritage to the society in which we now
live. In this chapter you will have the opportunity to examine some
insights from modern sociology and to raise questions for discussion
about how these ideas might impact your congregation.

They're only human

Certainly, everything the Bible tells us about the larger church—
and your congregation as a part of the church—is true, just as we saw
in chapter 2. The church is the people among whom the Word is

Text from page 181 of Wade Clark Roof's *Spiritual Marketplace: Baby Boomers
and the Remaking of American Religion* is copyright © 1999 by Princeton
University Press. Used by permission.

preached purely and the sacraments are administered in accord with the gospel. But your congregation is also a collection of people who are members of a society that exists beyond the church. Members of your congregation have a human side as well as a spiritual side. As Luther put it, we are "simultaneously justified, yet sinners." Therefore, it should not be surprising that the collection of people who gather together to form your congregation and to "do church" has much in common with other collections of people in this same society who gather together for other purposes.

In addition to its role as a community of Word and Sacrament, your congregation shares characteristics with service clubs, lodges, country clubs, social organizations, schools, hospitals, and charitable organizations of every type. Like these other organized groups of people, your congregation has to set certain rules, decide criteria for membership, make choices about finances, communicate with members, set goals, maintain property, and so forth. As unique as the church may be as the people of God, it is still a human institution.

See the "Congregational Model" on page 104 for a diagram of the three roles of a congregation.

This combination of attributes can sometimes be somewhat mysterious and rather confusing. In fact, much in the way that we speak of one God in three persons—Father, Son, and Holy Spirit—your congregation also has three faces: It is at once a community of spiritual formation, a voluntary association, and a non-profit organization. Each of these roles places demands on the congregation that can sometimes be in conflict with one another.

A community of spiritual formation

As noted in chapter 2, the congregation is a community of faith. In addition, a good deal of teaching goes on both formally (in classrooms) and informally (teaching by example). Young people and new members learn what the Christian faith is all about, sometimes in classrooms, but also by observing the living witness of the saints at work.

Sociologists refer to this aspect of a congregation as the *symbolic* level, because it is at this level that the uninitiated learn about the group's essential symbols. This means coming to understand both the meaning of certain signs—such as the cross, bread and cup, the font, and so forth—and how acts of charity, devotion, or piety symbolize our core beliefs. Our faith is symbolized, not only by the designs in our stained glass windows, but even more, by the actions of faithful people. So congregations are communities of people who engage in various symbolic actions, or who use certain symbols to communicate their beliefs to others. Thus, congregations are symbolic orders— communities of spiritual formation sharing the symbols of the faith through worship, education, and acts of love.

A voluntary association

At the same time, congregations are groups of human beings who come together not because they are forced or assigned to do so but because they choose to take part in common activities. In our society, individuals choose to belong to a congregation or not, and they choose which congregation they wish to belong to based on a variety of factors, of which common spiritual beliefs and symbols are only one. In most parts of North America, if a person doesn't like one congregation, for whatever reason, he or she can find another one close by—often of the very same denomination. Therefore, people associate with their congregations voluntarily, because they choose to do so.

Many organizations operate in a similar way. People interested in participating in a service club may be able to choose between the Kiwanis, Lions, or Sertoma clubs. Those attracted to lodges may choose between several orders, including Masons, Odd Fellows, or Eagles. We're used to having choices, and when it comes to finding a congregation, we go shopping for one we like.

Thus, every congregation, while functioning as a symbolic community, functions at the same time as a social group that, to a certain degree, competes with all other groups in the area. A congregation must, therefore, be intentional about how it engages people socially. A congregation must be concerned about how members interact, how they govern themselves, how they set group goals, and how they resolve conflicts.

As a voluntary association, it is a fact of life that not everyone will volunteer to associate. Some people will opt out, find another place that suits them, or relate less strongly to the group than others. No congregation can be all things to all people. It must, consciously or unconsciously, make choices about what sort of atmosphere it will establish, on what activities it will focus, and ultimately, to what kinds of people it will primarily appeal.

Because the gospel is for everyone, and Christ invites all people to come to him, there is a built-in conflict between the congregation's role as a community of spiritual formation and its role as a voluntary association. Yet, as groups made up of human beings, the reality is that congregations inescapably function in both roles—and in yet another, as a non-profit organization.

The three roles of a congregation also are discussed in *Called to Lead: A Handbook for Lay Leaders.*

A non-profit organization

A non-profit organization is a legally constituted corporation established for a particular purpose not directly related to business. Some examples of non-profit organizations include the American Cancer Society, the Society for the Prevention of Cruelty to Animals, and perhaps your local hospital and congregation. All of these share some things in common: They are all incorporated as legal entities that employ staff members, own property, and raise funds. They all have specific missions to which they devote all of their resources. Further, all of these non-profit organizations have relatively complex sets of formal policies and procedures that govern their day to day operation.

In the United States, non-profit organizations have certain legal responsibilities and receive certain legal benefits because of their non-profit status. Even though the First Amendment guarantees a separation of church and state, congregations must deal with the government at various levels. Federal tax regulations allow contributions to non-profit organizations to be tax deductible, but only if the organization's mission is not political in nature. Further, tax laws require such organizations to keep records of contributions and to issue statements or receipts that include specific details. State laws

**Every
congregation,
no matter how
small or how
large, functions
in these
three roles.**

usually require corporate registration in order for the organization to own property, and that corporate registration often requires the organization to establish a board of directors and to specify how members of that board will be selected. Local ordinances, such as building and fire codes, affect how non-profit organizations design office and meeting spaces, regulate traffic flow, and place limits on signs or other identifying symbols. Because congregations are non-profit organizations, they must comply with these various laws and regulations and manage themselves accordingly.

Thus, every congregation, no matter how small or how large, functions in these three roles—community of spiritual formation, voluntary association, and non-profit organization. Balancing and maintaining these roles will happen a bit differently in every congregation, but must be accomplished by all.

Three in One

Many congregations joke about the coffee hour after the service, or a regular potluck meal, functioning almost as an additional "sacrament" for members. Consider the typical church potluck as an example of how your congregation acts out its three roles:

- Someone had to arrive early to turn on the lights, prepare the room, and set up the tables. These people were serving the role of non-profit organization, seeing to facilities and procedures.

- Someone led those who had gathered in a table prayer before the meal began. This person was exercising the role of community of spiritual formation, leading an expression of faith.

- Someone else arranged for the program after the meal, and all enjoyed the talk around the table. These were functions of a voluntary association.

Similar dynamics could be pointed out for a committee meeting, a work day at the church, or a youth meeting. In nearly everything it does, your congregation lives out its three personalities simultaneously.

Boomers

Sociologists do not only study the nature of organizations but also the characteristics of the people who make up those organizations. Over the past 50 years, some changes have taken place in the attitudes and behaviors of people who make up congregations in North America. These changes follow well-documented trends but are not always widely reported or discussed. These trends are linked primarily to the baby-boom generation—those born in the generation immediately following World War II. Because this generation of Americans is so large in numbers, it has had a huge impact on the culture. Because this generation grew up in the post-war affluence of the 1950s and the cultural turmoil of the 1960s, that impact has also been unique.

Citing and summarizing the observations of many other social scientists, sociologist Wade Clark Roof notes that during post-war affluence there was a fundamental shift in how Americans came to define themselves in society. While traditional identities were rooted primarily in one's occupation (that is, what a person produced for society), since World War II, people have come to define their identities by what it is they choose to consume (lifestyle). The emphasis was no longer on finding ways to fit into the community, but on finding ways to distinguish oneself from the community, to become an individual. While some social critics consider this individualism to be the undoing of American culture, Roof maintains that the post-war economy simply brought to the surface tensions that were already part of the social undercurrent.

Added to the mix was the vast expansion and influence of the mass media. The result was both an increased awareness of other religious traditions and cultures, and the creation of what Stewart M. Hoover calls a "symbolic marketplace" from which individuals could customize their own sets of spiritual meanings as easily as they could change TV channels (*Religion, Media, and the Cultural Center of Gravity*, Center for Mass Media Research, University of Colorado, Address to the Trustees of the Foundation for United Methodist

Communication, May 7, 1998; available from www.colorado.edu/
Journalism/MEDIALYF/analysis/umcom.html). Boomers began to
question institutional authority, to drop out of traditional churches in
large numbers, and to significantly rewrite society's moral codes. This
trend has continued with the subsequent "X" or "buster" generation.

Because religious activity during the 1950s was very high in the
United States, most boomers had some experience in religious institutions during childhood. Currently, there is a trend toward boomers
returning to organized religion. Roof, however, disputes the notion
that this generation dropped its religious consciousness only to regain
it later in life. Instead, Roof maintains that spiritual issues have
always been on the minds of boomers, even if their religious practice
has taken different forms. He believes that it is important not only to
note that many boomers are now returning to church, but to know
why they are coming back and what they are seeking when they do.

Redrawing the boundaries

Roof's research with boomers on their religious journeys has led
him to suggest several basic types of religious and spiritual responses
among the baby-boom generation today. One type is the "secularist,"
the genuine agnostic or atheist whose life is ordered apart from religious or spiritual concerns. Roof notes that there have been secularists in every generation, and while their numbers among boomers may
be somewhat greater, they still represent a small minority.

Similarly, Roof identifies a group he calls "metaphysical believers."
These are the people often identified as New Age enthusiasts—people
experimenting with versions of the classical Eastern religions, believers in the power of crystals, nature worshipers, adherents to
re-inventions of ancient religions, and so on. Roof maintains that this
group is likewise very small, but has received media attention far out
of proportion to its numbers.

Roof's research demonstrates that the vast majority of boomers have
been believers in the faith in which they were raised. This faith has

not always found institutional expression in the same congregations or denominations of their youth. The largest shift has been from mainline to evangelical denominations. But even with this shift, "dogmatists" with fundamentalist beliefs and uncompromising moralism were in the minority in Roof's study of boomers. People considerably more open and flexible in their religious beliefs and practice made up the majority. Roof also found that views on politics or personal morality do not differ significantly across denominational lines between evangelical and mainline boomers.

A significant number of boomers—second only to the number of evangelicals—are satisfied in traditional mainline Protestant churches, seeking for their children the same sort of religious experience they enjoyed in their own childhood. These boomers, whom Roof calls "traditionalists," are looking for worship experiences involving formal liturgies and conventional hymns.

Thus, Roof and other social scientists note that there is a surprisingly consistent thread of traditional beliefs and practices among the adult population today. In addition, what differences there are in belief and practice often do not correspond clearly to institutional or denominational boundaries. Often in the same congregation, and certainly within the same denomination, it is possible to find people with an evangelical bent, mainline traditionalists, some dogmatists, some with interest in metaphysical beliefs, and perhaps even a few secularists (remember that a voluntary association can have people who belong for many reasons, some of them purely social).

> **The results of the work of sociologists are good news for congregational leaders.**

What does this mean?

The results of the work of sociologists are good news for congregational leaders. Things are not as bad as they have often been depicted for congregations today, because the majority of adults in our society are quite sympathetic to traditional religious beliefs. It is not necessary to win most people back from exotic beliefs into which they have strayed. These results also say very clearly that there is not a single type of potential church member in our society, nor is there a single recipe for attracting such people to a congregation. Because the young adult and middle-aged members of our society are a diverse group, they will respond to a diverse range of religious expressions, opportunities for spiritual growth, and ministry opportunities.

For example, because there are large numbers of boomers and "Xers" who are seeking vibrancy and enthusiasm in their religious expression, many congregations have had positive results with "contemporary" worship services. However, because there are also large numbers of individuals in these age groups who are seeking worship services much like those of their childhood, it is hardly necessary—in fact, it may be counterproductive—for every congregation to abandon traditional worship in favor of a contemporary service.

The variety of adults in American society suggests a variety of possible approaches to worship—as well as to education, witness, service, and fellowship. There isn't a single formula that magically will attract all of these people to a congregation. A congregation that attracts one type of person probably will not appeal to another type. Thus, no congregation can be all things to all people. The message from the scholars who study the sociology of religion in America is that congregations must first determine what types of people are most prevalent in their particular area, and discover what religious expressions, worship styles, and ministry opportunities would appeal to these people. The congregations then must take stock of their own resources to discover which of these expressions, styles or opportunities they are best equipped to supply. Only by specializing in doing those things you can do very well in meeting the needs of the people available to be served can your congregation be successful in outreach to its neighbors.

> **There isn't a single formula that magically will attract all of these people to a congregation.**

Continuing the conversation

As you gather with those who are concerned with the process of self-examination, begin as always with prayer. Thank God for the great variety of people in the world and for the gifts of knowledge, understanding, and discernment. Ask God to help you more clearly understand your congregation's roles as a community of spiritual formation, as a voluntary association, and as a non-profit organization. Above all, ask God to help you understand the special gifts your congregation has to reach out and minister to the particular types of people living nearby.

Questions for discussion

1. Create a list of the activities, functions, and tasks that volunteers and staff carry out in your congregation. Can you classify these into activities for "community of spiritual formation," "voluntary association," and "non-profit organization"? Into which category do most of your congregation's efforts fit?

2. As a voluntary association, what sorts of people choose to associate with your congregation at this time? How would you characterize your current members? How are these characteristics similar to or different from those of people living in the areas surrounding your congregation's building?

3. As a non-profit organization, what the most pressing issues your congregation currently faces? Brainstorm a list of matters related to budgets and finance, building and grounds, governance, and legal issues. How do these issues affect your efforts to be a "community of spiritual formation"?

Chapter 4

Constitutional Foundations

We, baptized members of the Church of Christ, responding in faith to the call of the Holy Spirit through the Gospel, desiring to unite together to preach the Word, administer the sacraments, and carry out God's mission, do hereby adopt this constitution and solemnly pledge ourselves to be governed by its provisions. In the name of the Father and of the Son and of the Holy Spirit.

—Preamble to the *Model Constitution for Congregations*
of the Evangelical Lutheran Church in America, 2001

An agreement among friends

Because they function simultaneously as communities of spiritual formation, as voluntary associations, and as non-profit organizations, congregations must make many decisions among their members. As a community of spiritual formation, members of the congregation must agree on the core beliefs and symbols that will be the foundation of its faith and teaching. As a voluntary association, members of a congregation must choose their common goals and objectives and agree on clear procedures for making day-to-day decisions and resolving disagreements with one another. As a non-profit organization, a congregation must fulfill legal requirements for handling funds, employing staff, and owning property. While it may be possible to simply make these decisions as various issues come up, experience has shown that decision-making is often easier and less prone to conflict when the key ground rules are agreed upon up front.

Such agreements have a long history. Archaeologists digging in Mesopotamia have unearthed the ruins of public buildings where thousands of contracts, written on clay tablets, were stored. In the

Old Testament, Abraham and the other patriarchs made formal
covenants with God or with one another. Some of the earliest
European settlers in North America paused to write a formal compact
before they disembarked from the *Mayflower* to begin building their
new home. More than a century later, delegates from the 13 original
U.S. states labored over a Constitution that would establish a new
nation. Whenever groups formally organize themselves, some sort of
governing documents usually are drawn up to state clearly the expectations group members have of one another. Often, as part of being a
non-profit organization, state laws require such a document to be
written and filed with the government.

Thus, a congregation's constitution is a record of its most fundamental agreements on its most basic decisions. It spells out who the
congregation is and what it is about, while fulfilling essential legal
requirements. At its core, the constitution is a contract that members
make with one another concerning their mutual responsibilities. That
is, it assures congregation members of what they should expect from
one another. This chapter will focus on the *Model Constitution for
Congregations of the Evangelical Lutheran Church in America.* If you
belong to another denomination, you will find many similarities here
with your own governing documents. Consult materials specific to
your denomination for details.

Where do constitutions come from?

The agreement between congregational members concerning their
most basic decisions about their mutual responsibilities is recorded in
the congregation's constitution. Because it is an agreement between
members of the congregation, it is not imposed on them from someone on the outside. However, because there are so many decisions
to be established for something as complex as a congregation, and
in order to fulfill all of its functions as community of spiritual formation, voluntary association, and non-profit organization, most congregations do not start from scratch. Instead, they choose a template

**A congregation's
constitution is
a record of its
most fundamen-
tal agreements
on its most basic
decisions.**

of some sort, making changes as necessary to address their own circumstances. Usually such a model is shared among congregations of the same denominational tradition.

The *Model Constitution for Congregations of the Evangelical Lutheran Church in America* is one such template. Each of the ELCA's predecessor bodies offered model constitutions to their congregations, and most of the bodies preceding these also offered models. Prior to these, many Lutheran congregations in the United States made use of models brought from founding churches in Germany or Scandinavia. A few ELCA congregations are still using constitutions based on older models with heavy modifications and amendments made over the years to adapt to the current situation. The danger of staying with an older document containing many amendments is that sometimes inconsistencies arise. If your congregation hasn't had a major overhaul of its governing documents in the last 15 years, it is probably overdue.

Congregations themselves are members of a larger body.

Another reason to use denominational models, aside from internal consistency, is consistency with the wider church. Just as members of a congregation agree together on basic sets of mutual expectations and mutual responsibilities through a constitution, congregations themselves are members of a larger body. In the ELCA, each synod and the wider church itself make up a "congregation of congregations" (Lowell G. Almen, *One Great Cloud of Witnesses! You and Your Congregation in the Evangelical Lutheran Church in America*. Minneapolis: Augsburg Fortress, 1997, p. 36). Each congregation, as a member of the churchwide organization, likewise agrees with other member congregations on certain basic expectations and mutual responsibilities. ELCA congregations are required, as one of the mutual responsibilities of their agreements with one another, to submit any changes to their constitution to their synod for approval. Again, the purpose is not to impose something on the congregation from outside but to assure that the congregation is abiding by its mutual understanding with the wider church, and to assist the congregation in avoiding inconsistencies or introducing legal problems into their documents.

Back to basics

The constitution, as the basic governing document of a congregation, is the most difficult to change of all congregational documents. Constitutions include the most basic agreements among members that the congregation wishes to keep unmodified over time. Somewhat less important agreements concerning the details of day to day operation of the congregation are recorded in other ways. (There is more to come on these.) Because the congregation is a community of spiritual formation, the constitution includes a statement of the faith it teaches. The *Model Constitution for Congregations of the Evangelical Lutheran Church in America* begins with a brief chapter that gets some legal requirements out of the way, then goes directly to a more detailed chapter summarizing the congregation's Confession of Faith. This chapter, and the one that follows on the nature of the church, are mandated—that is, required for all congregations who wish to belong to the ELCA. To disagree with these is to question the essence of the faith as taught in the ELCA. These chapters in the constitution proclaim the congregation's adherence to the Bible and the Lutheran confessions.

Constitutions include the most basic agreements among members that the congregation wishes to keep unmodified over time.

A sense of purpose

Constitutions of Lutheran congregations in North America have, for many decades, set forth a five-part purpose: Worship, teaching and learning, witness or evangelism, service to those in need, and the nurture and support of members. To this traditional list the ELCA's *Model Constitution* adds "preserve unity" (C4.02.f.) as part of the congregation's purpose. It's important to look at this constitutional segment and some discussion questions in detail.

> C4.02. To participate in God's mission, this congregation as a part of the Church shall:
>
> a. Worship God in proclamation of the Word and administration of the sacraments and through lives of prayer, praise, thanksgiving, witness, and service.
>
> —*Model Constitution for Congregations of the Evangelical Lutheran Church in America*, C4.02.

In keeping with the Lutheran confessions, Word and Sacrament are first on the list of the congregation's purposes. However, the *Model Constitution* goes one step beyond the confessions by suggesting that a congregation's worship should spill over into members' lives through daily prayer and devotional acts ("praise, thanksgiving") and also through witness and service.

• In what ways does worship life lead to witness and service in your congregation?

> b. Proclaim God's saving Gospel of justification by grace for Christ's sake through faith alone, according to the apostolic witness in the Holy Scripture, preserving and transmitting the Gospel faithfully to future generations.
>
> —*Model Constitution for Congregations*, C4.02.

Certainly proclaiming the gospel can occur in any number of ways or settings, but this section of the *Model Constitution*'s purpose statement places emphasis on purity of doctrine and study of Scripture for adults, and teaching the faith to children ("future generations"). The congregation's educational ministries for both adults and children are the primary means of proclamation in this context.

• What are the particular strengths of the educational ministry of your congregation?

• What aspects of your congregation's educational ministries need to be strengthened further?

> c. Carry out Christ's Great Commission by reaching out to all people to bring them to faith in Christ and by doing all ministry with a global awareness consistent with the understanding of God as Creator, Redeemer, and Sanctifier of all.
>
> —*Model Constitution for Congregations*, C4.02.

When it comes to witness and evangelism, the congregation is challenged to "think globally" and "act locally." The congregation is to be a vital witness to the faith locally through its own ministries and intentional evangelism. The congregation also supports the work of evangelists in far off places.

- In what ways does your congregation regularly act to specifically evangelize your local community?
- In what ways does your congregation raise its own awareness of global mission?

> d. Serve in response to God's love to meet human needs, caring for the sick and the aged, advocating dignity and justice for all people, working for peace and reconciliation among the nations, and standing with the poor and powerless, and committing itself to their needs.
>
> —*Model Constitution for Congregations*, C4.02.

When it comes to witness and evangelism, the congregation is challenged to "think globally" and "act locally."

This is a tall order! In this section of the purpose statement the congregation is confronted with all of the world's needs, from the sick or elderly next door to world peace among the nations. Clearly, no one congregation can address every human need and concern around the world, or even all the needs in a local area. But this provision of the *Model Constitution* insists that just because the needs are great, the congregation cannot give up. Each congregation will fulfill this purpose in its own way. In its bylaws, and most particularly in its mission statement (to be discussed in more detail shortly), the congregation needs to define precisely those needs it will address in its own community, and those worldwide concerns on which it will intentionally focus.

- Which needs has your congregation identified as its primary concerns locally?
- Which needs has your congregation identified as its primary concerns globally?

> e. Nurture its members in the Word of God so as to grow in faith and hope and love, to see daily life as the primary setting for the exercise of their Christian calling, and to use the gifts of the Spirit for their life together and for their calling in the world.
>
> —*Model Constitution for Congregations*, C4.02.

Nurture of members implies various forms of pastoral care, including visitation of the sick and infirm, counseling of the troubled, and ministries of healing and wholeness. It's important to note that "pastoral care" is not done only by pastors. Rather, this provision of the purpose statement of the *Model Constitution* calls for members of the congregation to use their gifts to exercise their own ministries in daily life.

Not only are members nurtured by the congregation, but they nurture others, as well.

Nurture goes both ways—not only are members nurtured by the congregation, but they nurture others, as well. Part of this nurturing is through the support of ministries carried out by and for others in the congregation. Thus, even as they are supported by the congregation, members support the congregation through stewardship of their gifts.

• Who are some of the people who nurture members of your congregation?

• What ministries of healing and wholeness are carried out by your congregation?

• In what ways is your congregation nurtured by the gifts of its members?

> f. Manifest the unity given to the people of God by living together in the love of Christ and by joining with other Christians in prayer and action to express and preserve the unity which the Spirit gives.
>
> —*Model Constitution for Congregations*, C4.02.

In the prayer he prayed with his disciples on the night before his death, Jesus prayed that all his followers might be one (see John 17:20-23). Despite the obvious factions and divisions in the one holy catholic and apostolic church, Christians take this prayer for unity seriously. Unity is made manifest in loyalty to our own denominational congregation of congregations, and also in loyalty to one another as congregational members. Unity is particularly fostered in dealing positively with conflicts and in showing due respect to congregational leaders.

This chapter of the ELCA's *Model Constitution* goes on to enumerate specific tasks all congregations will do to fulfill their purpose, but the constitution specifically gives each congregation wide latitude about how it will organize itself and carry out its tasks. Organizational decisions are recorded in other governing documents of the congregation and are not included in the constitution itself. The constitution also requires the congregation to adopt a mission statement that includes the congregation's specific purpose in its unique time and place.

Also speaking to the congregation's role as a voluntary association, the *Model Constitution* includes sections concerning membership, some key committees, and other structures. Finally, because the congregation is a non-profit organization, the constitution also has articles spelling out the congregation's relationship with its pastor(s), detailing legal issues of property ownership, setting rules for congregational meetings and election of Congregation Council members, and approving constitutional amendments.

All of these basic decisions remain essentially unchanged over long periods of time and therefore are recorded in the constitution itself. There are other decisions congregational members make that are not always of such lasting importance.

Other governing documents

Many decisions made by congregational members should not be part of the constitution because they may be subject to change more frequently than might be convenient through the constitutional amendment process. Two other means are available for formally adopting and recording congregational decisions. These are bylaws and continuing resolutions.

It's in the bylaws

Decisions that need to be made by the entire congregation, but are likely to need changing more frequently than those included in the constitution of the congregation, are recorded in the form of bylaws.

The congregation's members can alter bylaws at any appropriately called congregational meeting.

Bylaws vary greatly from congregation to congregation. Sometimes they are in a separate document from the constitution, with its own numbering system, while other congregations choose to integrate each bylaw into their constitution so that a bylaw regarding the congregation council, for example, would appear at the end of the article of the constitution that discusses the congregation council. Nearly any congregational decision can be included in the bylaws so long as that decision is not in conflict with the constitution. Often these decisions will provide the broad outlines of an organizational structure, details of when congregational meetings will be held, and so forth.

Keeping the corporate memory

Less critical matters of policy, which can be delegated to the congregation council to decide, are recorded in continuing resolutions. Continuing resolutions are not considered or ratified by the congregation as a whole. However, continuing resolutions may not be in conflict with either the constitution or the bylaws of the congregation. Unlike a congregational resolution or a congregation council resolution—each of which expresses an opinion or intention at a given point in time—a continuing resolution continues until it is rescinded.

Statements of mission and purpose

For more on congregational mission statements, see *Our Mission: Discovering God's Call to Us.*

While the ELCA's *Model Constitution* lays out the purpose of the congregation in general terms that apply to all congregations, each congregation has a particular mission which it defines for itself in light of its understanding of the needs of the community it serves and the gifts it has been given. A congregational mission statement should be a paragraph that describes what the congregation does precisely enough that it would not apply to any other congregation.

Sometimes there is confusion between a mission statement and a slogan. Congregations sometimes adopt a single phrase as a slogan, much as a business adopts a slogan for advertising purposes. There's nothing wrong with having a slogan. In fact, a catchy phrase that people remember can be very useful in raising congregational visibility. But a single catch phrase can't be specific enough to describe the unique ministry of the congregation in its particular context.

Each congregation has a particular mission.

Continuing the conversation

As you gather with those who are concerned with the process of self-examination, begin as always with prayer. Thank God for the great variety of people in the world and for the gifts of knowledge, understanding, and discernment. Ask God to help you more clearly understand your congregation's roles as a community of spiritual formation, as a voluntary association, and as a non-profit organization. Above all, ask God to help you understand the special gifts your congregation has to reach out and minister to the particular types of people living nearby.

Questions for discussion

1. Read your congregation's constitution and bylaws. Are there any surprises? Do these documents accurately reflect how your congregation is structured and how it carries out its mission today?

2. How seriously does your congregation take its six-fold purpose of worship, proclamation, outreach, service, nurture, and unity? Which of these does your congregation do best? Which would you like to see strengthened?

3. How up to date are your congregation's bylaws and continuing resolutions? What provisions might need to be changed or amended in order to allow for or encourage new ministries?

4. What is the unique mission of your congregation as described in its mission statement? Does the statement clearly describe your congregation only, or is it a generic description that could apply anywhere? What are the unique ministries that might be included in your mission statement?

Chapter 5

Understanding Our Community

But seek the welfare of the city where I have sent you into exile, and pray to the LORD on its behalf, for in its welfare you will find your welfare.

—Jeremiah 29:7

What is our neighborhood?

The purpose statement in the *Model Constitution for Congregations of the Evangelical Lutheran Church in America*, which we explored in chapter 4, speaks in some grand terms about the congregation's mission. It includes phrases like "global awareness," "reconciliation among the nations," and our "calling in the world." But to be completely practical, the world is a pretty small place for your congregation and its members. Despite the ongoing need to think in global terms, congregations must act locally. Determining the locus of that action is what this chapter is about.

Every congregation has a definite and limited sphere of influence. A congregation can only do so much, and can only carry its ministry so far. True, through the work of partners in the "congregation of congregations" we call the wider church, that influence can (and should) extend beyond the usual horizons. But to be the best possible stewards of their resources, congregations need to recognize those horizons and concentrate their local ministry efforts within them. Defining a "service area" in which the congregation will focus its primary efforts is a critical step. It helps the congregation decide just how much it can bite off at one time, and it sets parameters beyond which the congregation can legitimately say, "That's someone else's job." Defining a service area helps the congregation establish its responsibilities clearly without over-extending itself.

Defining the congregation's service area

Most often, a service area is defined in terms of geography, although some alternative definitions will be considered later in this chapter. A geographic definition of a congregation's service area is sometimes natural and self-evident. If your congregation is located in a small town, it is likely that the primary service area is that town and the rural areas surrounding it. Sometimes congregations in urban areas find themselves situated in distinct neighborhoods that form a primary service area. If your congregation exists in such a readily distinguishable community, the first step of this process is easy to accomplish.

Many congregations, however, are not located in places with such clear definition. Moreover, it is common for congregations to make assumptions about the geographic area they serve and then to be surprised to learn that their service area is actually wider or narrower than they imagined.

Generally, the same barriers that deter people from crossing from one place to another in their daily social or business activities also prevent the crossing of those barriers to attend worship or to participate in a ministry program. The stereotype about "living on the wrong side of the tracks" is not far from reality. A railroad, river, major roadway, municipal boundary, or other geographic feature can have a profound effect. So even if the congregation thinks that its ministry extends beyond such a boundary, the people on the other side may not see it that way.

Conversely, a major transportation link, such as a primary street or road, a bus route, or train line that people regularly travel in the course of daily activity may extend the congregation's natural reach. People who routinely drive a particular route to work or school during the week may, out of habit, be comfortable traveling that way

> Defining a service area helps the congregation establish its responsibilities clearly without over-extending itself.

Geographic
features are
a powerful
factor in
determining the
limits of a
congregation's
outreach,
but they are not
the only factor.

on a Sunday morning or at other times for church activities. At the same time, they may be reluctant to travel even a shorter distance from home in a different direction, because it just doesn't feel natural.

One good way to get an idea of the area a congregation currently serves is to obtain a local area map and to indicate the location of each member household with a pin or other marker. If the majority of pins cluster in a particular area, a de facto service area appears. If relatively few pins are found on the other side of a geographic barrier, this indicates that the congregation's ministries are unlikely to penetrate that barrier without a great deal of effort. If the cluster of pins tends to trail out along some major transportation artery, such that the congregation's worship location is off the center of the cluster, this is a clear indication of habitual travel or other factors.

Geographic versus non-geographic areas

Use the
"Determining
Your Service
Area" tool on
pages 105-106 to
identify the
zip codes in
your area.

Geographic features are a powerful factor in determining the limits of a congregation's outreach, but they are not the only factor. Just because a bunch of pins creates a cluster on a map doesn't mean that the congregation's ministry excludes anyone residing outside the cluster, nor does it mean that every person residing within the geographic service area will be a good fit for the congregation's ministries.

For example, if a congregation were to initiate a worship service in a language other than English and begin an intentional outreach program to an immigrant population that speaks that language, the congregation's service area might become geographically wide and scattered. But the congregation would nevertheless focus on a particular area of specialization. Similarly, if a congregation were to determine that its ministry should focus on the needs of single parents, or blended families, or the elderly, and so forth, the congregation's geographic service area would be altered significantly by such a decision.

The trick is to strike a balance between the realities of geography and resources versus the extent of Christian love and concern. A congregation might have a deep concern for inner-city Hispanic immigrants and desire to launch a Spanish language ministry. But if that congregation happens to be located in an affluent, outer-ring suburb many miles from the inner city, that ministry is unlikely to be very fruitful. Similarly, if a congregation in a rural area is experiencing a rapid decline in the number of family farms and a rise in the average age of the population as young people move to the cities, it will be difficult to launch a vital youth ministry.

Congregations need to focus their ministry in a way that will allow them to utilize their gifts effectively. But they also need to be realistic about the kinds of ministry that can be done within their locale. This can only be accomplished by taking a good look at who the congregation's neighbors actually are.

Congregations need to focus their ministry in a way that will allow them to utilize their gifts effectively.

Finding out who lives here

No congregation can be all things to all people, nor should any try. By first determining at least a rough geographic area, then by looking carefully at what sort of people live there and what sort of needs those people have, a congregation can fit its ministries to an area of service.

Often, congregations assume that they know who their neighbors are. Congregations assume that their neighborhood is much as it always has been, or that the neighbors are just like the members themselves. But as neighborhoods constantly change, congregations need to periodically reassess their circumstances. Because businesses and governments are also interested in understanding the clientele in any given area, information is readily available about the current residents of nearly any neighborhood.

Demographic data

An essential way to begin to understand the people in your congregation's service area is to acquire and interpret demographic information, just as businesses, service organizations, and government agencies do when planning their work. Some information, such as income levels, may be difficult to obtain, but having demographic data on hand and keeping it current can be helpful for planning in your congregation. A church database software program can make compiling the data much easier.

Demographic data quantify the attributes of a group of people. Once attributes such as age, gender, and education are reduced to demographic data for people in your service area, you can compare your congregation and service area with others, identify what is typical for your area by calculating the *mean* (average) or *median* (half higher, half lower), or *mode* (most frequently occurring number), spot trends over time, discover unique aspects of your community, and generate charts and graphs to interpret the information and present it to others.

Describing individuals in terms of numbers can seem cold and impersonal, but by looking at people in this statistical way, you can develop a fuller understanding of your congregation's opportunities for ministry. Knowing, for example, that half the people in your service area are substantially over or under the median age for your county, state, or nation will help you decide whether to invest your energies in discussing ministries for people nearing retirement or for parents of preschoolers. The "Examining Our Service Area" tool on page 107-108 provides you with a template for making comparisons between your congregation, community, county, state, and the nation regarding total population, gender, racial or ethnic identity, age groups, types of households, and some aspects of socio-economic level.

The U.S. Census Bureau makes demographic data available to the public, either for sale or for free. This data is collected not only through the census carried out every ten years, but through ongoing sample surveying and other methods. Spend some time at the Census Bureau's Web site (www.census.gov) to see what is available, including summary reports down to the county level. Please note that blocks and tracts are the smallest units described. Information about individuals or households is not available. Also, by law the Census Bureau cannot collect information about individuals' religious affiliation.

For most congregations, the most useful demographic data will be at the zip code level. If your primary service area includes more than one zip code, run a separate report for each one and then combine the numbers. If your congregation has a secondary service area, prepare a separate set of demographics for that area. Discuss the possibility of funding a new mission congregation or establishing a satellite congregation to serve what is now your secondary service area.

Information at the zip code level can be obtained from companies that have the sophisticated software needed to put the raw census statistics together in different ways. The Evangelical Lutheran Church in America (ELCA) purchases demographic information at the zip code level and then makes the information available at no charge. If you are in an ELCA congregation, enter your synod and congregational identification numbers at the Department for Research and Evaluation's Web site (www.elca.org/re) for access to this information. Additional reports also are available at this site, including your congregation's reported statistical history and a survey-based estimate of religious affiliation in your county. You will need to run separate reports to obtain the state and national comparative figures. If you are not in an ELCA congregation, check to see what information is available through your denomination. Government (municipal or county) planning offices or local agencies also might be willing to share census information that they have purchased.

Because demographic data that is available for free usually requires additional analysis and interpretation, many marketing companies sell a repackaged version of the information that is easier to interpret. This information often includes indications of changes that are apparent over time, ways that your area is significantly different than other geographic areas, identification of dominant or overlooked groups of people in your area, and so on. One company that customizes information for congregations is Percept (www.perceptnet.com), but other market research firms offer similar packaging of demographic data. Be sure to carefully define your primary (and secondary, if any) service area and shop for the best price before making a purchase of this kind.

Demographic trends

A key component of any interpretation of demographic data is trend analysis. A set of statistics from a single survey is really only a snapshot of an area at one moment in time. Census data and statistical reports often show percentage changes in various demographic measures over the previous decade, or some other time frame. Sometimes these reports offer estimated projections of how a certain demographic parameter will change in the future, if present trends continue. Knowing not just how things are in the neighborhood, but also how they are changing, is invaluable for congregational planning.

Although understanding how things are changing in your neighborhood is vital for congregational planning, it is important to remember that statistics do not provide a crystal ball that can look into the future. If the previous decade shows a particular trend—for example, an increase in the number of young families or of Spanish speaking immigrants—that trend may or may not continue. Sometimes a trend has run its course by the time it becomes evident statistically. It is also possible that some unanticipated factor will intervene, such as an economic boom or recession, a change in government policy, a major new construction project or some other fundamental change in the neighborhood. Demographic trends often are a congregation's best way to anticipate what ministries might be developed in the present to reach fruition in the near future. Nevertheless, if ministries are developed in response to perceived demographic trends, it is best to monitor demographic data to be certain that the trend is unfolding as anticipated.

Psychographic data

In addition to demographic data that is easily quantified, a complete understanding of the people your congregation serves is impossible without a clear idea of their values, attitudes, and lifestyles. There are many questions about how people live, how they think, and the way they feel about things that are not always discernable from demographic data alone. Many businesses have come to understand that it is not enough to simply know the ages, incomes, and education levels of potential customers. Attracting customers also means knowing how people spend their time and what ideas and activities interest them. Politicians have become keenly aware that voters' positions on issues do not necessarily correlate to demographic categories, and so they need to find ways to listen to individual viewpoints. Congregations, too, because they deal with matters of the spirit and not with sales and profits, need to know more about the people they wish to serve than can be told with numbers.

This *psychographic* data is gathered through survey techniques and usually is reported in aggregate form. This type of information frequently is called *polling data*, because it seeks the opinions of respondents rather than factual data, such as age or education level. By designing survey questions that probe for attitudes and feelings on various subjects, and then calculating what percentage of respondents feel a certain way, questioners can learn the range of attitudes on a particular subject, and the distribution of opinions along the range.

Further, by linking psychographic data to demographic responses, questioners can draw conclusions that are correlated to particular demographic characteristics. For example, the responses might show that most women feel a certain way about a particular subject, while most men have the opposite opinion. Or, people in a particular age group might tend to hold one pattern of opinions while people who are older or younger might tend to have somewhat different opinions on the same subject.

The power of psychographic data

Businesses today sometimes use sophisticated methods to obtain psychographic data on their customers. You probably have been asked to complete product-warranty cards that inquired about your interests and how you spend your free time. Large retail chains entice shoppers to apply for some sort of membership card. The card application asks for a great deal of demographic data, including address, age, gender, and income level. Attractive discounts are offered to entice shoppers to present their card each time they make a purchase. The store's computers are then able to make complex associations between particular shoppers and particular products. By tracing buying patterns, businesses are able to determine, for example, that women under age 30 are more likely to buy product "A," while men over 50 will prefer product "B." With this information, the store is able to develop advertising campaigns or promotions targeted specifically to the customer who is most likely to buy a certain product.

Congregations, of course, do not alter their doctrines according to psychographic data. Nor do they attempt to sell products or offer discount cards. However, some commercial suppliers of demographic data will also supply some psychographic data on the population of a congregation's geographic service area. This information can be very helpful in ascertaining whether people in the service area will be receptive to the congregation's outreach, and can suggest points of faith and doctrine to emphasize.

Even more, psychographic data can point to some underlying needs that may exist within a community. By understanding the lifestyles of people who live in the service area, congregations may be able to guess what is missing from those lifestyles that the congregation can supply. For example, if the demographic data show large numbers of households with young children, and in which both spouses are employed full time—and the psychographic data show an attitude of frustration with busy schedules and too few hours in the day—it may suggest opportunities for child-care programs, nursery schools, and family oriented ministries that will structure quality time for families to spend together. If demographics indicate large numbers of young single adults in the service area—and psychographics show concern over safety after dark or lack of safe places in which to socialize—it may suggest opportunities for singles ministries or service projects that can help neighborhood cohesion.

Although the collection and interpretation of psychographic data can be an extremely complex art and science, the addition of psycho-

Psychographic data can point to some underlying needs that may exist within a community.

graphic data can greatly enrich a congregation's understanding of the social dynamics of the service area and provide deeper insight into the mind-set of the individuals residing there. However, there are ways the congregation can go beyond psychographic information to really get in touch with people in the service area. These methods will be discussed in detail in chapter 6.

Continuing the conversation

As you gather with those who are concerned with the process of self-examination, begin as always with prayer. Thank God for the opportunity to reach out to a unique community of individuals with varied characteristics and viewpoints. Ask God to help you better understand the people in your congregation's service area. Above all, ask God to help you understand the special gifts your congregation has to reach out and minister to particular types of people, and to help you discern exactly what your area of service should be.

Questions for discussion

1. Where do most members live? Does the pattern of residences of current members suggest the approximate boundaries of a geographic service area for your congregation? Does it differ from what you expected?

2. What are the demographic characteristics of the people living near your congregation's worship location? Do they differ from what you expected?

3. What trends are evident in the demographic data for the area near your congregation's location? What ministry opportunities can you see in these trends? What current ministries of your congregation will no longer be appropriate if present trends continue?

4. If you have access to psychographic data for people in your area, do any needs emerge that might be met through some congregational program?

Chapter 6

What Do Our Neighbors Expect from Us?

You should do good to all people, help them and promote their interests, however and wherever you can, purely out of love to God and in order to please him, in the confidence that he will repay you richly in everything.

—Luther's Large Catechism, Part I,
Robert Kolb and Timothy J. Wengert, eds., *The Book of Concord*
(Minneapolis: Augsburg Fortress, 2000), pp. 430

Undertaking a neighborhood canvass

As valuable as demographic and psychographic data may be, they seldom provide a complete picture of everything you ought to know about the people in your congregation's service area. If you are fortunate enough to have access to very good psychographic data, you may have an adequate understanding of the people you wish to serve. However, the best psychographic profiles can provide only a general picture of how your congregation might offer ministries that will directly impact people's lives.

Truly understanding the deeper spiritual needs of people in your community requires knowledge of how people think, feel, and act. The best way to do this is to take the time to actually talk to people. Market researchers and public-relations firms approach this task very methodically, using interviews, focus groups, and other techniques. Congregations can approach this task less formally and still learn a great deal about the people within their service areas.

This chapter will suggest one informal technique for gathering information from people in the service area—a modified interview approach called a neighborhood canvass. Some alternative information gathering techniques will also be discussed.

What can be learned from a neighborhood canvass?

The purpose of the neighborhood canvass is to meet some of the people behind the numbers who come through the demographic and psychographic profiles and to discover ways the congregation might directly reach out to them through ministries that meet specific needs. While demographic data can supply important information about the age, gender, income, education, and family status of the residents surrounding your congregation, it reveals very little about the deeper hopes and needs of individuals. While psychographic data can supply information about the issues that many people in an area feel are important, it furnishes only limited insight into the circumstances and emotions behind those attitudes. Only by taking the time to really talk to some of the people represented by the survey numbers can congregations genuinely understand what the statistics mean. Only through understanding can truly effective ministries begin.

One caution is in order: At least since the 1950s, congregations frequently have used the canvass, or "religious census," as a thinly veiled excuse to knock on doors and persuade neighborhood residents to attend church. Be clear that the primary purpose of this canvass is not to speak, but to listen. The main objective is not to create a list of unchurched people, but to identify the needs of the community. Invitations will be in order once the congregation has listened to those needs and developed new ministries as a result.

Sampling

It is unlikely that your congregation will have enough available people to canvass every home in the service area. Professional researchers make use of sampling techniques to cut down on the number of contacts that must be made to provide accurate information. Your canvass need not be scientific in order to provide information

The primary purpose of this canvass is not to speak, but to listen.

for congregational planning. You can get the job done with informal sampling.

Sampling allows researchers to interview relatively few subjects, but to project the results to a much larger population, at least within certain margins of error. Creating a statistically valid sample is a laborious process, but for the canvass you need only approximate information. The exact way of determining the sample is unimportant. The critical thing is to find some way of ensuring that the contacts you make in the canvass aren't all concentrated in one place and that they don't exclude some parts of the area, but are distributed more or less evenly throughout the area so that a good mix of different types of households is achieved.

Keep the purpose of the canvass clearly in mind.

Developing canvass questions

See pages 109-110 for suggestions on how to effectively sample your neighborhood.

As you prepare to canvass a sample of the people residing in your congregation's service area, keep the purpose of the canvass clearly in mind. You are not going out to win converts—you are going to learn from your neighbors how the congregation might serve them in ways that will bring the gospel into their lives. You are not contacting your neighbors in order to preach to them, but in order to listen to them.

With this in mind, you can prepare a short list of open-ended questions for the canvass. The list of questions is short because the goal is to get people talking freely. However, canvassers will need to listen carefully and be able to think on their feet to come up with follow up questions that probe more deeply into the responses they receive. Demographic and psychographic data have already furnished the factual information. This phase of the study needs to get behind the facts to the underlying emotions or convictions that lead individuals to certain beliefs, attitudes, or ways of seeing the world.

In *Revitalizing Church and Community: A Resource Manual for Faith-Based Organizing*, by David L. Ostendorf and Paul R. Peters (pp. 33-34), the Center for New Community, a faith-based research, training, and advocacy organization in Chicago, suggests that an effective canvass can be conducted using just three questions.

- What do you like about our community?
- What are the needs or concerns you have about our community?
- How do these needs or concerns affect you personally?

These questions can provide volumes of information. First, begin with a brief and well-rehearsed introduction explaining the purpose of the canvass, and follow up with well-focused questions. By beginning with the positive, the three questions set an upbeat tone to the rest of the discussion. By opening the door to concerns the participants are free to express a wide range of issues, from petty complaints to deep social or personal problems. By asking participants to name ways in which these concerns affect them personally, petty complaints can be short-circuited, freeing the canvassers to go back and ask about concerns until issues of personal consequence emerge. (For additional information on the Center for New Community, see http://www.newcomm.org.)

Ways of conducting the canvass

A neighborhood canvass can seem like a daunting task, and even the most dedicated congregational member can turn timid at the thought of walking up to a perfect stranger to talk about matters of faith and life. The temptation may be great to take some sort of short-cut, or to look for ways to talk to only people with whom we feel safe and comfortable. Even worse, the congregation may try to avoid talking to anyone in the area at all, and simply call their own assumptions about the neighbors "good enough."

Mail

A canvass can be conducted by mailing a questionnaire to a number of households in the area. However, great care must be taken in the design and wording of the questionnaire, a stamped self-addressed reply envelope must be included, and the rate of response will be extremely low. Perhaps one out of every 100 questionnaires will actually be completed and returned. This is a poor return on the investment necessary for the mailing, and except under rare and difficult circumstances it is not good stewardship.

Telephone

A useful canvass can be conducted by telephone. This is less expensive than a mailed questionnaire, assuming the canvass area is within a local calling district and a list of phone numbers of households in the specific service area is readily available. Response rates will be somewhat better, with perhaps one call in 10 resulting in a response. For this method, use a very well-written script explaining the purpose of the call and a nearly professional telephone questionnaire.

Door to door

However, there is simply no substitute for talking to people face to face. While the level of receptivity to a visitor at the front door will vary greatly, visitors usually are surprised to discover that strangers are willing to talk quite a bit once some basic trust is established. This trust is more quickly achieved in person than by phone or other means. Response rates for door to door canvasses usually range from 70 percent to more than 90 percent.

Canvass visits generally work best when one member of a two-person team takes the lead in conducting the interview, while the other takes notes and asks follow-up questions as appropriate.

In analyzing the conversations, observers need to sharpen their eyes and ears to watch closely and listen "between the lines." The purpose of the canvass is not just to gather opinions about the topic under discussion, but to look for what aspects of the topic elicit more animated or emotive responses. You don't just want to know how people feel, but why they feel that way—the underlying beliefs, attitudes and motivations. This helps you understand the person you are canvassing—and the other area residents whom they represent—on a much deeper level than is possible with a simple survey.

Alternative techniques

In rare cases, an area canvass is simply impossible to conduct either in person or even by telephone. There are some alternative means of listening to the people in your neighborhood that are usually more difficult to accomplish effectively or do not yield results that are as reliable. However, in some cases these may be the only alternatives available. Sometimes these techniques can be used as a supplement to the canvass to gauge the receptiveness of residents to a specific potential ministry or program.

Focus groups

A focus group is a focused discussion on a topic of interest that is conducted by a trained leader. The discussion typically is held in a comfortable room just large enough for the discussion participants, but which allows for the discussion to be observed by additional researchers and recorded for further analysis later on. Ethically, of course, participants must be informed that their conversation will be observed by others. Focus-group participants are sometimes selected from a given area at random. Other focus groups are composed of people specifically selected to represent certain demographic profiles. Gifts or other incentives are usually used to encourage group members to participate and to compensate them for their time.

If a congregation has a member or members trained in focus group techniques, such a group drawn from residents of the congregation's service area could yield valuable information. It is important to have a clear focus in mind before the conversation begins—hence the term *focus group*. Such a focus might be general, such as "What needs might a Christian congregation address in the neighborhood or area?" Usually, however, the focus is more specific, such as "Would families in this area be better served by a church sponsored day-care center or a church-centered preschool?" The key is to make participants comfortable enough to speak, while keeping the conversation focused on the topic of interest.

Continuing the conversation

As you gather with those who are concerned with the process of self-examination, begin with prayer. Thank God for the great variety of people in the world and for the gifts of knowledge, understanding, and discernment. Ask God to help you more clearly understand your congregation's roles as a community of spiritual formation, as a voluntary association, and as a non-profit organization. Above all, ask God to help you understand the special gifts your congregation has to reach out and minister to the particular types of people living nearby.

Questions for discussion

1. Now that you have had the opportunity to review the available demographic and psychographic data for your congregation's service area, what is still unknown about the people who live within the reach of your congregation? What do you still need to learn about them?

2. As you look at available demographic and psychographic data, what ministries or programs appear to best serve the residents of this area? How might you double-check to see if these ministries would truly meet the needs of residents?

3. In your canvass of a sample of the residents, what issues or concerns have been identified? How do these concerns match up with those you anticipated, based on the demographic and psychographic profiles? What ministries or programs appear to be most needed in light of these expressed concerns?

4. What surprises have you discovered among the expressed concerns of residents in your area?

Chapter 7

Our Congregation Today

Examine yourselves to see whether you are living in the faith. Test yourselves. Do you not realize that Jesus Christ is in you—unless, indeed,
you fail to meet the test!

—2 Corinthians 13:5

Who are our members?

By now, you and the other members of your steering group know a
great deal about the people who live in the area your congregation
seeks to serve. You have defined that area. You have gathered demographic and psychographic profiles of the people residing in that area.
And, perhaps with assistance from other volunteers, you have talked
face to face with a representative sample of the area's population, gaining insights into their joys, dreams, concerns, and frustrations.

Perhaps you are now getting a fairly clear picture of a variety of
ministries or programs through which your congregation might reach
out to these people to serve them and to help meet their expressed
needs. By bringing a measure of healing to some of the problems and
concerns they have identified, your congregation has the potential to
bring the kingdom of God near to them. As you proclaim the gospel
in actions that are relevant and vital, you will create opportunities to
witness directly to the loving mercy of Jesus Christ as Savior.

But before becoming too excited about the possibilities of serving
these new friends and neighbors that you've only just met, it's time to
take a step back and look at just what gifts and resources your congregation has available for such ministries. It is time, as Jesus said, to
count the cost (Luke 14:28). The gifts and resources are not simply
physical or monetary, but include the time, talents, and energies of

individuals within your congregation. The costs, likewise, are not just money, but the costs to other ministries and other opportunities.

In this chapter, you will have the opportunity to count some of these costs and begin an inventory of some of your available resources. In chapter 8, you will have the opportunity to begin planning for resources that are currently missing but can be developed over time.

Understanding our heritage

The legacy of a congregation's past is one of the most significant factors affecting its present readiness for ministry.

The legacy of a congregation's past is one of the most significant factors affecting its present readiness for ministry—and one of the least understood or appreciated factors as well. The circumstances of a congregation's founding and the significant events of its past are all part of its unique heritage. These are more than historical artifacts, but are frequently keys to understanding why the congregation does things they way it does today, and how it might react to the idea of doing something new tomorrow.

For example, some congregations in the Midwest and West were founded by immigrant groups forced to flee oppressive church structures in northern Europe about 150 years ago. A number of these congregations continue to maintain an instinctive distrust of churchwide (denominational) and synodical (regional) institutions and structures. In these congregations, even current members, who may have no ethnic or cultural ties to the founding members, learn subtle cues as they are socialized into the congregation. Members continue to hold these attitudes even if they do not know the history from which they stem. It is simply part of how that congregation has lived and worked for more than a century, and it is part of the personality or corporate culture of the congregation.

Meanwhile, some other congregations in the East and Midwest were founded by immigrant groups that came from parts of Scandinavia, where direct participatory democracy was highly valued. These congregations often have four or more congregational meetings each year with very long agendas. Again, the roots of the practice in history may be lost, but in these congregations there is a strong part of the corporate culture that says, "We should all have a vote in every decision that is made."

The personality of a congregation is shaped not only by its founders but also by significant people and events through its history. A congregation that once had a pastor who betrayed its trust by sexual indiscretions or mishandling congregational funds may carry in its personality a distrust of pastors—even if the incident occurred decades ago and present members have no personal memory of it. Such feelings can become part of a corporate culture that is passed on to later generations.

Additionally, congregations sometimes are divided by long-past disagreements. A sense of who is on "our side" and who is on "the other side" may carry over into other issues and decisions. Similarly, a major event, such as a move to a new building location, can become an unconscious point of division, with members who belonged to the congregation before the event forming one faction, and those who joined the congregation after the event forming another.

Patterns of thinking and feeling often change much more slowly than external circumstances. Ways of making decisions or handling conflicts and disagreements are learned. People often react to situations based on ways they learned to handle what they perceive to have been similar situations in the past. Often the roots of these reactions begin beneath the conscious level. Therefore, a careful study of a congregation's history is often helpful in coming to an understanding of how things got to be the way they are today.

The personality of a congregation is shaped not only by its founders but also by significant people and events through its history.

Explore your congregation's history with the tool on page 111.

Locating demographic trend data

Some important aspects of a congregation's history are reflected in the congregation's demographic records. Numbers of baptized and active adult members, average attendance at worship services or Sunday-school classes, amounts received through offerings and amounts given to certain causes are figures that most congregations calculate and record at least annually. Usually these records are maintained over very long periods of time. Significant changes in any of these statistics usually point to some significant changes taking place at that point in time.

As discussed in chapter 5, the ELCA Department for Research and Evaluation (http://www.elca.org/re/) makes demographic data concerning their surrounding communities available to ELCA congregations. Congregational demographic histories are also maintained and available at no charge through this unit of the churchwide offices in easy to use reports on membership, attendance, and general giving.

An analysis of demographic trends within your congregation can give you a unique picture of what is happening.

Just as you looked at demographic trends for your potential service area in chapter 5, an analysis of demographic trends within your congregation can give you a unique picture of what is happening. Is membership increasing or decreasing? Is the percentage of members in attendance on an average Sunday going up or down? Look at the ratio of adult members to all baptized members, which is an indication of the number of children and the average age of the congregation's members. If the ratio is increasing, the average age of the congregation members is growing older. If the ratio is decreasing, the number of children in the congregation is increasing.

Granted, it is possible to place too much emphasis on demographic trends as an indicator of congregational health. Some congregations grow in depth of commitment and understanding of the gospel while declining in membership or attendance. However, the demographics are a good and fairly easy place to start examining the congregation.

What are we doing?

As you consider taking on new ministries or programs that are designed to reach the needs of residents of your service area, it is also important to examine the current ministries of the congregation. Congregational leaders often feel that this step is unnecessary because they already have a good understanding of what is going on in their congregation. However, many are surprised by the scope of ministries—or by what is missing—when all activities are listed and displayed in one place.

Taking a ministries inventory

Take a look at your congregation's current ministries. Conduct this ministry with at least the self-study steering group present, if not a wider group of congregational members. This is because no individual, in even the smallest congregation, can know all of the things that members are doing in all areas. Working in a group to complete an inventory of congregational ministries provides the benefit of a wider perspective.

See the "Ministries Inventory" tool on page 112.

The primary purpose of this inventory is to discover what areas of ministry might already be in place that could be expanded or modified to encompass the potential new ministry opportunities you have discovered within the service area. A secondary purpose is to assist you in identifying essential ministries that are not being carried out in your congregation, or ministries that are being done poorly that should be improved.

Levels of congregational satisfaction

In addition to listing the various ministries and programs presently being carried out by your congregation, it is important, as well, to evaluate these programs. Listen to members to hear their attitudes about what is important to them about the congregation and how potential new ministries might fit into their dreams for the future. At a minimum, you will want to talk informally with some of the key people involved in each ministry area of the congregation, and to learn from them their honest opinions and constructive criticisms of the ministries currently underway. How do members of the choirs feel about worship? How do Sunday-school teachers feel the congregation's educational ministries are going? Have goals been set for evangelism and service in the congregation, and have these goals been met?

One way to gather this information is to ask each ministry team, committee, or board within the congregation to devote one meeting to frank and open discussion with a member of your steering group about what is going particularly well and what could use improvement in their area of responsibility. The self-study process could encourage such an evaluation on a regular basis—perhaps setting aside one regular meeting annually for this purpose. But in this case, the steering group member's notes will supply you with information about levels of satisfaction with the congregation's programs at this moment in time.

Truly evaluating programs and ministries, however, involves not only the leaders of such programs, but all who benefit from them. Therefore, it is highly desirable to conduct a much wider listening effort in the congregation.

> **No individual, in even the smallest congregation, can know all of the things that members are doing in all areas.**

Seeking input from congregation members

In the same way that you looked at psychographic data for the residents of your service area and sampled the residents in a canvass in order to listen to their joys and concerns, spend some time and energy listening carefully to the present members of the congregation. By hearing what members value most about their congregation, leaders can avoid making changes that upset large numbers of people. By understanding the dreams, ambitions, and motivations of present members, leaders can begin to see how the congregation can be energized for service and how the needs of the neighborhood might fit with the willingness of the present members to engage in action and outreach. In other words, in these conversations you are trying to find ways that the potential ministries you have identified among residents of the service area might match up with the potential energy of congregational members.

Some congregational leaders resolve to invite each family unit of the congregation to a personal 30-minute interview for this purpose, which is a laudable goal. Other congregations invite congregational members to participate by scheduling several group sessions over the course of a week or two, and encouraging members to sign up for a

One congregation coupled a series of congregational interviews with appointments for photos for a new pictorial directory. As each member household came in to be photographed, the adults were asked to complete a brief psychographic questionnaire. After the photos were taken, a member of the self-study steering committee met with each family unit for 10 or 15 minutes of focused conversation about the congregation and its ministries.

session at a time convenient for them. These sessions are facilitated by a designated leader in much the same way as a focus group.

However the process is handled, the goal is to focus on and listen carefully to members' joys and concerns. Three questions could be asked:

1. What do members value most about their congregation—why do they choose to belong?

2. What concerns do they have about the congregation now, and about future of the congregation?

3. How do those areas of concern affect each member personally?

Spend some time and energy listening carefully to the present members of the congregation.

Be sure to have someone record responses as the discussion leader or interviewer concentrates on follow up questions that help probe for the underlying feelings and attitudes that lead to the opinions expressed.

As you analyze the responses from members, try to reach a clear understanding of what core values are the foundation for your congregation's life together. What are the things about the congregation that most members consider to be so fundamental as to be beyond question or challenge? Also, what are the common threads that hold the congregation together? Is the congregation bound by family ties? By a common ethnic heritage? By common loyalty to a particular person (perhaps a person in the past, such as a particularly dynamic former pastor)? By a particular ministry or program? Or is there some other bond that attracted these people and holds them together?

Also, listen for shared definitions and meanings associated with common terms. What do words like *mission, ministry, community,* and *outreach* mean to members of your congregation? There often is wide diversity among the shades of meaning of these terms, and communication is difficult until common understandings are negotiated. For example, when people in your congregation hear the word *mission,* do they think in terms of what their congregation does locally, or only in terms of the work of the denomination or of overseas missionaries?

Try to reach a clear understanding of what core values are the foundation for your congregation's life together.

Listening carefully for common understandings of these and other words and phrases used to talk about the work of the congregation and the wider church will be an important part of the process of understanding the present members of the congregation and preparing for the interpretation of new goals and opportunities. An effective communication process will depend on a clear understanding of the way language is used among congregational members.

Continuing the conversation

As you gather with those who are concerned with the process of self-examination, begin as always with prayer. Thank God for the people who have been called together into your congregation, with all of their many hopes, dreams, aspirations, and interests. Thank God, too, for the many vital ministries in which your congregation is engaged, and the faithful people whose giving of themselves allows these ministries to take place. Ask God to help you more clearly understand one another and to communicate effectively. Above all, ask God to help you understand the ways in which your congregation can become even more effective in witness and service.

Questions for discussion

1. What events and people brought your congregation into being? What stories have been passed down as part of the folklore of your congregation's founding?

2. What have been the major turning points in the history of your congregation? How do these historical turning points continue to mark the congregation with a living legacy in the way your congregation lives and works today?

3. Do the demographic patterns of your congregation over the years reflect significant events and forces? Are there sudden changes in demographic trends in the historical statistics that seem to have no explanation? What may have caused these changes?

4. What are the signature ministries or programs of your congregation? What things does it do better than any other congregation around? What are the sources of pride among the members?

5. What gaps are there in the congregation's ministries? Who is not being served, or not being served as well as they ought to be?

6. What is the glue that holds this congregation together? Where are the cracks between groups that sometimes disagree or come into conflict with one another?

7. What sort of language do the members of your congregation use when they talk about their church? What are the shades of meaning they attach to their words?

Chapter 8

Our Congregation Tomorrow

Beloved, we are God's children now; what we will be has not yet been revealed. What we do know is this: when he is revealed, we will be like him, for we will see him as he is. And all who have this hope in him purify themselves, just as he is pure.

—1 John 3:2-3

What are our strengths?

Understanding your congregation's current ministries and the attitudes of present members is a good foundation for the launching of new efforts to reach out to people in your service area. Building on that foundation will require some careful planning. In this chapter you will learn to evaluate your present resources for ministry and assess what will be necessary in order to initiate new or newly revitalized ministries. In addition to physical and financial resources, you will consider your intangible and human resources as well.

A common way of planning is called *needs assessment*. With this approach, a hospital administrator might find that a certain number of hospital beds usually are needed for a population of a given size, count up the beds available in the area, and discover that there are 10 percent fewer beds than needed, thereby identifying a deficiency in the community. Recently, planners have begun using Asset Based Community Development (ABCD). In the above situation, this approach would focus on the possibility that there are already other service providers in the area or ways to make people healthier, thereby reducing the number of beds needed. This might lead to a strategic alliance with an underused convalescent center or to collaboration with parish nurse programs in local congregations rather than a construction program to provide more beds at the hospital.

Asset based planning in a congregation looks not only at what is wrong, missing, or deficient but at the gifts the congregation already has been given and assets close at hand that could strengthen its work (for example, "Two people are willing to teach half the time" rather than "No one will teach the fifth grade class every week").

Physical resources

Most congregations are property owners. The vast majority of congregations in North America hold title to a piece of real estate and have one or more buildings dedicated permanently and full-time to the ministry of that particular congregation. For most congregations, the church building and grounds are the largest—if not only—capital investments and tangible long-term assets. It is likely that your congregation allocates a significant proportion of its annual budget to the care and maintenance of this property. Good stewardship demands that your congregation receives a good return on its investment, and that property assets are used to the maximum benefit of the congregation and those it serves.

How does your congregation understand the function of its building and grounds? Members of congregations traditionally approach

See the tool "More Than Enough: An Asset-Based Planning Process" in *Our Stewardship: Managing Our Assets.*

In the Midwest, the rural economy is changing rapidly. While a farm of 160 acres often supported a large family a couple of generations ago, a farm of 1,000 acres barely supports a typical family today. Rural populations have diminished, and many small towns no longer have enough people to support businesses, schools, or churches.

As membership numbers decline, many open-country and small-town congregations struggle to hang on. Numbers are so small that all available resources must be directed toward maintenance of the facility. By the time bills are paid for heat, lights, and basic upkeep, there is nothing left for mission.

Perhaps there is no longer a pastor, church staff, Sunday school, or even the most basic programs. Yet the members remain committed to using their re-sources for the building alone. When this happens, the building becomes a monument to ministries that no longer are being carried out.

In many cities, once-thriving neighborhoods are now run down. Vibrant communities of immigrants once founded equally vibrant congregations in these neighborhoods, and working class families sacrificed much to support church buildings where they could worship and children could be instructed in the faith.

Now, the grandchildren and great-grandchildren of these immigrants have moved to the suburbs. But on Sunday mornings they faithfully drive into the old neighborhood to worship at the old church. The building is well-maintained through the generous support of these now middle-class descendants, and there is adequate support for staff and programs.

But often the current residents of the neighborhood—who may be of ethnic groups from succeeding waves of immigration—are welcome in the building only if they come on the congregation's terms. Speaking Spanish may be frowned upon in places where worship was once conducted in German or Swedish. Such places are museums of a noble heritage, but current opportunities for ministry in the neighborhood may be missed.

How does your congregation understand the function of its building and grounds?

their property from three perspectives: *monument, museum,* or *machine*. Understanding and acknowledging the perspective most of your congregational members have relative to the church building will help you gauge how open the congregation will be to utilizing its building and grounds for new types of ministry programs.

Some congregational members see their church building as a *monument*. They view it in the same way that one might regard a headstone that marks the burial place of a loved one. The monument is to be maintained in pristine condition because it symbolizes and memorializes something important from the past. Monuments generally are not changed unless the change is absolutely necessary. A primary goal is to minimize any actions that may increase wear of the monument and cause it to require additional maintenance, thus it is best to keep it off-limits to unnecessary traffic except when memorial services are being held.

Perhaps the largest group of congregational members regard the church building in much the same way they might regard a *museum*.

Like the monument, the museum is dedicated to the past. Unlike the monument, however, its purpose is not so much to symbolize and memorialize the past as it is to educate and indoctrinate others into the heritage. Younger generations and newcomers are invited—indeed, encouraged—to come inside, view the exhibits, and participate in the educational programs so they might better appreciate and identify with the common heritage preserved here. In the museum model, changes are sometimes needed to keep the facility attractive and to do the job of cultivating and passing on a living culture. Expansions are necessary as new chapters of the congregation's past unfold and need to be interpreted. Remodeling must occasionally occur so that the museum keeps up with the latest and best ways of transmitting the culture to others.

Some congregational members will regard the church building in much the same way one regards a *machine*. Machines are acquired to fulfill a specific function—a manufacturing company may purchase a machine to stamp out widgets, a farmer purchases a tractor with which to till the ground and plant crops, or an individual buys a car to provide transportation. The machine exists to serve its owner, not the other way around. It is understood from the outset that the machine is

A mission congregation, less than 10 years old, has just moved into its "first unit," an attractive but hardly ornate structure consisting primarily of a large, open multipurpose room.

Chairs are set up in rows for Sunday worship, partitions divide the space for classes later on Sunday morning, and three mornings each week the entire space is converted into a nursery school operated for neighborhood preschool children.

When a planned addition is constructed, this space—where dozens of babies have been baptized—may become a fellowship hall, or it may be divided into functional rooms separated by permanent walls.

The only consideration is how to best use the space to serve the ministries of today and tomorrow. This facility is a machine, but one from which the congregation is getting great mileage.

a means to an end, and not an end in itself. The oil will have to be changed regularly, worn parts have to be replaced, and when things break—as one must expect that they will with constant use—they must be repaired. All of this is just part of the overhead of owning and operating the machine.

The machine has a useful life, and while one will certainly maintain the machine carefully in order to extend that useful life as long as possible, it is accepted that the day will come when it must have a complete overhaul. The machine is about the present, not the past. We may become attached to it, and shed a tear on the day we have to trade it in, but most people replace it nevertheless.

Clearly, the healthiest attitude toward the church building for a congregation devoted to mission and ministry is the machine model. New mission congregations almost always regard their new facilities in this way—few new congregations set out to build monuments. But over time, emotional attachments become strong as significant life events—baptisms and confirmations, weddings and funerals—take place in church buildings. A natural human instinct is to preserve important memories by attaching them to physical objects. A clear understanding of how congregational members view their building—as a monument, museum, or machine—will help you tailor a proposal to that understanding for using the building in a new way for a new ministry.

Give careful consideration to how the physical space available can be adapted to the ministry program you envision. Some programs, such as day-care centers or preschools, will have to meet special fire and safety codes. Research the special requirements for the program you have in mind by contacting the fire department or building inspector for your area. Understand the consequences of the proposed ministry for your building—what areas will be subject to additional traffic and therefore additional wear and tear, and what modifications or remodeling will be required. Be forthright with your congregation about these consequences. If your church building is not suited to these needs—or if resistance among congregational members is too great—give consideration to alternative locations that might be rented.

A congregation in a Midwestern city happens to be located next to a major, multi-lane freeway, just at the point where the freeway takes a sharp bend. It is a very prominent location, because drivers are looking right at the church building in their windshields as they make the turn.

However, there is no exit from the freeway at that point. To actually reach the church requires driving a half mile farther, then doubling back on a complex maze of one way streets.

Thousands of drivers know that church's location, and recognize its name from a well-placed outdoor sign. But very few could actually find their way to it, should they be inclined to try. On the traffic level, the church is inaccessible.

Visibility and accessibility

Certain attributes of your congregation will have an impact on potential ministries that is difficult to measure, but nevertheless very real. The most significant aspect of a congregation's image is usually its visibility in the community. The most visible thing about a congregation is often the building and grounds. If the building is located in a very visible location—at a major intersection or along a main street—most people in the area will be aware of its existence. If the church building is a well-known landmark, the location can be a powerful asset in launching a new program. Closely associated with the location of the congregation's facilities is accessibility. There are three levels of accessibility to consider: *traffic access, entry access,* and *perceived access.*

Traffic access involves how easy it is find the building and drive to it by car. Adequate parking also makes a place accessible to those who have driven to get there, and should be considered as part of your building's traffic accessibility. If your location is easy to get to and parking is available nearby, you have an asset.

Entry access, or accessibility on the entry level, is also an issue for buildings that have multiple entrances. If the main entrance is not appropriately marked, first-time visitors may have a very difficult time finding the right door to enter. Some people may simply give up. And of course, steps and other obstacles will make the building entry

The most visible thing about a congregation is often the building and grounds.

inaccessible to those who must use a wheelchair. Entry accessibility can usually be enhanced with simple signs, ramps, or lifts. If these things are already in place, you have an asset.

Perceived access is more difficult to define and evaluate, as it entails how psychologically easy it is for those who have never been there before to walk inside. Anything that makes entering the building intimidating can be a barrier to access, while an inviting building is an asset. Having a building location that is widely known and readily recognized and accessible in all respects is a great asset.

Congregations sometimes are able to make themselves more visible in the community. Using various forms of advertising sometimes can create this visibility. One well-placed billboard or relatively inexpensive box ads in a local weekly newspaper can create name recognition. If a pastor or another congregation leader happens to have a talent for writing insightful letters to the editor concerning various community issues, these can also be a tool for creating name recognition. Congregations in small towns and rural areas usually have greater access to local media than do urban congregations. Small-town newspapers are hungry for news, and small-market radio stations often will provide free air time for well-produced programs. If your congregation has made itself visible through local media in the past, this is an advantage. If not, it's not too late to begin. For a more complete discussion of using the media to increase congregational visibility, see the resource kit *Go Public! Developing Your Plan for Communication Evangelism* (ISBN 6-0001-1775-2), available through Augsburg Fortress.

Financial resources

Because of the nature of the congregation as a voluntary association, perhaps no topic is quite as difficult as that of money and finances. Yet, as a non-profit organization, and even as a community of spiritual formation, financial resources are essential. As a congregation anticipates launching new forms of outreach to its service area, there can be a great sense of excitement about doing something new that translates into generosity in financial giving.

Christians are called by God to be good stewards of what they possess. This stewardship is exercised both individually and corporately. Just as individual members are challenged to manage their resources so that a portion is shared with the congregation, the congregation must manage its resources appropriately. When congregations do so, and individual members see that the money they give is used efficiently for purposes they support, some level of increased generosity will inevitably result. Thus, every effort should be made to make congregational budget decisions openly and consistently, with adequate input from all voting members. Further, congregations must be intentional about reporting financial information to members and interpreting the information in ways that help members understand how spending relates directly to the congregation's mission. When you are up front in speaking about money, you create an asset.

Occasionally, the euphoria of a new ministry opportunity may lead congregations to become overly optimistic about finances. This is especially true if the introduction of new ministries is associated with a major fund-raising campaign in the congregation, campaign results may inspire spending on the new programs before money is actually received. Most professional fund-raisers acknowledge *slippage*, or a difference between amounts pledged and amounts actually contributed, of between 5 and 10 percent. If you see such slippage, don't be discouraged. Giving trend data from your congregation's demographic profile can provide an indication of income expectations so that you can plan appropriately.

Depending on the nature of the proposed ministry program, "seed money" may be available from a charitable foundation or other grant-giving institution. If there is a foundation in your local area that frequently supports social service agencies, grants might be made to the congregation if the proposed ministry program meets the foundation's criteria. You could also contact your synod office or other regional judicatory concerning the availability of special grants from denominational or fraternal sources.

For more on stewardship of resources, see *Our Stewardship: Managing Our Assets*.

One caution, however, about grant funding: The granting agency will expect a written proposal that meets very precise criteria, and will likely require even more precise written reports detailing how the funds were spent. If you have members of your congregation who write grant applications as part of their work, you will want to consult these people extensively on how to go about the process.

When you are up front in speaking about money, you create an asset.

Calculate the necessary expenditures for the ministry program you are considering. Consult with others with expertise in similar programs about hidden or unexpected costs. Be completely forthright with your congregation and its leadership about the anticipated costs of the program, and be prepared with options for funding sources.

Intangible resources

The greatest asset your congregation can enjoy, of course, is a positive reputation among the people of the community it serves. A long tradition of active service through the congregation's ministries becomes widely known by word of mouth. If your congregation enjoys such a reputation, you are fortunate to be able to build on it. If such a reputation has not yet emerged for your congregation, the ministries you are currently planning can help to establish it.

Human resources

The sort of reputation described above can come about partially through building facilities and partially through programs, but primarily, what makes a congregation special will be the people who represent it in the course of their daily lives. Your congregation's people are its greatest resource. In previous chapters, this book has mentioned congregation members who might have expertise or experience with some skill through their daily work. However, most congregational ministries are carried out by people who simply have been called by the Holy Spirit to respond to the good news of the gospel. You will certainly want to make note of members of your congregation with special gifts, particularly as they relate to the new ministries you hope to initiate. Every person with a passion for the mission of the church can be utilized in some way to further the congregation's work. There are two keys:

1. Fitting the right job to the right person.

2. Offering invitations to ministry tasks in such a way that the person can accept.

First, find out about members' interests, skills, and backgrounds so that you can match each member with a task appropriate to his or her abilities. Don't be afraid to challenge people with opportunities for service that might be new to them, but try to maintain an inventory of interests and skills for each member. Many inexpensive computer database programs available today will enable such an inventory to be kept in an easily searchable form.

Second, when inviting members to give of their time for a particular service, try to tailor the invitation to make it as easy as possible for the member to give an affirmative response. In our busy society, this frequently means asking for short-term commitments and perhaps teaming two people who can trade off on the same task. If a member declines an invitation to serve in some way, ask them for honest feedback concerning what is causing them to feel apprehensive about making the commitment. If possible, revise the invitation to make the task more suitable to this member, or to other members you may later approach.

Your congregation's people are its greatest resource.

Whatever you may need

As you consider the new ministry initiatives that will meet the needs you have discovered in your service area, and as you assess the resources available in your congregation now, you may discover that additional resources will be necessary. List these needs, and creatively consider how you will find the facilities, finances, and people that will make your plans a reality. Think about sources for these resources that have not been tapped in the past. Brainstorm alternative ways of accomplishing the plan with resources already available. With imagination and ingenuity you can accomplish your ministry goals. The trick is to focus on how to use the resources you have, not to be paralyzed by what you lack.

Continuing the conversation

As you gather with those who are concerned with the process of self-examination, begin as always with prayer. Thank God for the many gifts of your congregation. Ask God to help you see and use these gifts to reach out and minister to the residents of your service area.

Questions for discussion

1. How do most congregational members regard your church building? Do they see it as a monument, museum, or machine?

2. What will be the implications for your congregation's building if you go ahead with new ministries that you envision at this time? Who in your community can advise you about necessary changes to meet new ministry needs?

3. What have been the trends in financial giving in your congregation? How has financial information been shared with members and how have spending decisions been made?

4. What costs will be associated with the new ministry initiatives you are considering? What alternative sources of funds are open to you?

5. How accessible is your congregation's building to the community? Is it accessible to traffic? Are the entries well marked and accessible to all? How inviting is your building to newcomers?

6. How can you use the local media to increase the visibility of your congregation?

7. What are the specific roles or tasks that will need to be fulfilled in order to carry out your ministry plans? Who are the people available to carry out these tasks?

Chapter 9

Where Do We Go from Here?

We have no mission but to serve
In full obedience to our Lord;
To care for all without reserve,
And spread his liberating Word.

—from "The Church of Christ in Every Age,"
text by Fred Pratt Green, *Lutheran Book of Worship* 433

A new vision for ministry

Your steering group has worked long and hard to learn about your congregation and the community where it is located. You've examined biblical and confessional foundations of mission, constitutional models, demographic and psychographic profiles of the service area, and feedback from congregational members. The members of the steering group probably have a clearer understanding of your congregation and the challenges and opportunities before it than any other group in the congregation. The members of your steering group probably are also more excited about the potential you have discovered for your congregation's future than any other group in your congregation.

The task before you now is to translate what you have learned and the vision you now see into a clear and workable strategy for the congregation. You must interpret this strategy, your rationale for it, and your enthusiasm about it to the rest of the members of your congregation. This chapter will assist you with these tasks.

Establishing objectives

This book presumes that as you have studied the residents of your service area and considered the gifts available to your congregation for ministry, the Holy Spirit has opened your eyes to seeing new ministries your congregation could carry out to bring the kingdom of God near to your neighbors. As a steering group, you undoubtedly have talked about common dreams for what your congregation can do in this area. Because of the needs you have discovered, your goal may be, for example, to begin a special ministry to families or to the elderly, or a day-care center, or a food pantry, or worship services in Spanish, or a contemporary service—or any of 100 other ideas that have come to you through your study. But there are several steps between saying what you want to do and making that a reality.

Develop SMART goals.

Develop SMART goals. Useful goals are *specific*, not general. They identify who, what, when, where, why, and how. Goals should be *measurable*, dealing with things that can be counted such as tangible objects or observable human behavior. Goals should be *attainable* within the time allotted to achieve them, using the resources available. Goals should be *realistic* so that they have a direct effect on the situations they are meant to address. Don't set as your objective "eliminate all poverty on the entire planet by next week"—unless you have billions of dollars available! Goals also should be *timely*, appropriate to the things that matter most now.

A *measurable* objective provides a clear indication of when and how well it will be accomplished. "Get some singers together" is not a very *specific* or *timely* objective. However, "Recruit six competent singers to lead contemporary worship by August 1" is measurable—if you have at least six singers by August 1 you know your objective has been met, but if you only have four by that date, you know the objective has not been met. Establish a set of SMART objectives that will take you from your vision to realizing your goal. Brainstorm the steps necessary: gaining approval, securing funds, recruiting personnel, and so forth, in order. Be certain that the time line is practical.

Building a strategy

A strategy is a set of steps necessary to achieve defined objectives. For each of the objectives you have established, strategies address the questions: *Who? What? When? Where? Why? How?*

For example, if the goal is to establish a neighborhood preschool and the objective is to hire a certified preschool director by April 30, one strategy might be that George *(who)* will place a classified ad *(what)* for next Sunday's edition *(when)* of the local newspaper *(where)* to seek applications from candidates *(why)*. The *how* section might be left to George in this case, or it might specify what the words in the ad should say, how the billing for the ad should be handled, or how George is to report that he has accomplished his mission.

Goals, objectives, and strategies are used every day, whether to accomplish grand visions for ministry or just to run family trips to the grocery store. We don't always call them by these names, nor do we always write them out so clearly. However, when members of a group are coordinating complex activities over time, much frustration and missed communication can be avoided with this level of detail in planning objectives and carrying out strategies.

A strategy is a set of steps necessary to achieve defined objectives.

How do we share what we've learned?

A major challenge is to share what you have learned and the opportunities you have discovered with the leadership of your congregation. Because your steering group is already composed of a number of key congregational leaders and represents a cross section of the congregation in terms of age, gender, and concerns, you already have a head start in sharing your new knowledge and your new visions for ministry with other leaders. The challenge for your steering group now is to find ways to share your insights, ideas, and enthusiasm in ways that will cause the enthusiasm to be contagious. You need not only share information with others, but also share inspiration and excitement.

Reports

Written reports, such as those that appear in the congregation's annual report or in mailings sent to members to keep them advised about the self-study process and its results, are particularly useful in presenting factual information. Written reports can be used throughout your congregational study process to provide the congregation with summaries of your findings. These reports, however, are less effective in conveying enthusiasm and excitement. In any case, the reports need to be very concisely written—in our busy world, few people will read more than a single page at a time on any given topic, and a half page is even more likely to be read.

Writing clear and concise prose is an undervalued skill. Choose the person in your steering group who has the most training and experience in writing to write the first draft. But let that person rely on others to read and reflect on the draft, and offer suggestions. Reports should be a group effort in the sense that one person does the writing, but others offer editorial suggestions so that key pieces of information are conveyed clearly and succinctly.

Presentations

Oral presentations, such as those made in a Sunday morning "mission message" or "temple talk," or as an oral report at a congregational meeting, are opportunities to make excitement and enthusiasm contagious. The amount of factual information that can be effectively communicated verbally is limited to main themes and key points. Oral presentations are appropriate from time to time throughout the study process, but particularly as the process begins, and again as the process moves toward recommending particular ministries and identifying new opportunities.

You need not only share information with others, but also share inspiration and excitement.

Again, not everyone can speak effectively and enthusiastically before a group in public. Effective public speaking is a skill, and the people within your steering group with the most training and experience in speaking are probably those best equipped to communicate in this way. Additionally, visual aids, such as charts, graphs, or posters, can enhance an oral presentation if they are used well. However, presenters should avoid the temptation to overwhelm an audience with visuals. Presentations should inspire first, and inform second.

Toward that end of inspiring the audience, an oral presentation must not be just standing up and reading a written report. Oral language and written language are not the same. While an oral presentation should be well planned and rehearsed, it should be delivered in a style as natural as a conversation between good friends. If the oral presentation is going to convey excitement, the person giving the presentation needs to be excited about the topic.

Newsletters

Most congregations have some form of newsletter that is periodically mailed to all member households. Too often these newsletters are large and infrequent, rather than brief and numerous. In our busy society, newsletters must compete for the brief moments of attention readers have to give them, amid a flood of mail received each day. A well-crafted, single-sheet, weekly newsletter is much more likely to be read than a multi-page monthly or quarterly booklet.

As you prepare content for your congregation's newsletter, keep articles brief. Your congregation's newsletter can be a very effective tool for helping members of your congregation understand the information you are learning in your study process, and for introducing them to specific ministry proposals.

How do we get the paperwork in order?

How does the congregation actually consider and adopt new ministries, and how does it reorganize itself to undertake these ministries effectively? As discussed in chapter 4, congregations order themselves by adopting certain documents, most frequently bylaws and continuing resolutions. The language of these documents is usually rather formal. However, the ideas behind bylaws and continuing resolutions can be communicated in reports, presentations, and newsletter pieces prior to their consideration at congregational meetings or by the congregation council. The adoption of appropriate documents is important in itself, as it represents the way in which congregational decisions are made and recorded. More importantly, the process of considering these documents helps congregation members to clarify their understanding of the information that has been learned, and build enthusiasm for new ministries.

Congregational decisions

As noted in chapter 4, decisions that are so important that they need to be made by the entire congregation, but are likely to need changing more frequently than those included in the constitution of the congregation, are recorded in the form of bylaws. Bylaws can be altered by the congregation's members at any appropriately called congregational meeting. However, no bylaw may conflict with any article of the constitution.

If the study you have conducted leads you to suggest that your congregation take a new direction or embrace a fresh perspective, placing a new mission statement before the members in the form of a bylaw is a way to focus attention on this new direction. By adopting this bylaw, the congregation invests in the new ministry opportunities before it.

In proposing a new mission statement or any other new bylaw, be sure to make use of newsletters and presentations in advance of the congregational meeting where it will be considered to inform members about the proposal and to build enthusiasm for it. Help members understand the need for such a new direction and grasp your excitement about the new opportunities.

Another means of placing new visions before the entire congregation is through a congregational resolution. Such resolutions are largely symbolic in their effect, but they offer the congregation the opportunity to formally consider a course of action and to go on record as endorsing it. Such a resolution may state the congregation's intent to enter into prayer and study on an issue, or may direct its council or other leaders to carry out certain instructions. The process of discussing and considering bylaws or resolutions helps the congregation discern God's will, aside from the resulting actions.

Writing continuing resolutions

Continuing resolutions, as described in chapter 4, are considered and adopted by the congregation council. It is usually not necessary for these resolutions to be considered or ratified by the congregation as a whole. Continuing resolutions are particularly useful for establishing the details of a congregational structure.

By creating a separate continuing resolution for each committee, board, or ministry team, the congregation council delegates its authority to each of these groups. By including a complete statement of responsibilities and expectations for each committee, team, or board, the congregation council communicates to the members of each group exactly what its task will be. Because the congregation council can change these job descriptions at any time, there is maximum flexibility to make adjustments as necessary.

As you consider the ministries you wish to carry out, and the purposes mandated by your constitution, think about what tasks need to be addressed and how those tasks can best be divided among various groups. Some creativity here is a good thing. Don't create groups just because it seems like you ought to. Instead, create them around specific sets of responsibilities. Because the purpose of the church is mission, and not to create committees and meetings, serious consideration should be given to allowing the form to follow function. Consider what needs to be done—the functions that are essential to carrying out your mission goals—group them together in ways that seem appropriate, and create a committee, team, or board for each group of tasks.

For more details on mission statements, see the book *Our Mission: Discovering God's Call to Us.*

Now what?

Congratulations! You've done it! You've studied your service area and the gifts and resources available to your congregation. You've decided on new ministry goals, and you're beginning to develop SMART objectives and detailed strategies. You have prepared the necessary documents and secured congregational approval. Your entire congregation now shares the results of what you have learned, and the

Another means of placing new visions before the entire congregation is through a congregational resolution.

enthusiasm that you've generated. Only two things remain: celebration and communication.

Find a way to celebrate what has happened with some sort of festive activity. Thank God, thank one another, and enjoy the pride of a job well done. Invite the whole congregation to share in the excitement of the new mission taking shape. Invite the whole neighborhood—publicize it as widely as possible, and use the event to draw attention to the new thing God is doing in your midst. Use the event and other avenues of communication to let residents of the service area know what your congregation is doing for them. Pull out all the stops to make your new ministry visible in the community you serve.

Continuing the conversation

To read more about organizing for mission and ministry, see the book *Our Structure: Carrying Out the Vision.*

As you gather with those people who are concerned with the process of self-examination, begin as always with prayer. Thank God for the great variety of people in the world and for the gifts of knowledge, understanding, and discernment. Ask God to help you more clearly understand your congregation's roles as a community of spiritual formation, voluntary association, and non-profit organization. Above all, ask God to help you understand the special gifts your congregation has to reach out and minister to people living nearby.

Questions for discussion

1. What steps will be necessary to bring about the goals you have for ministry? How can a *specific, measurable, attainable, realistic,* and *timely* (SMART) objective be written for each of these steps?

2. What means are available to communicate your goals and objectives to other members of the congregation? How can you help them catch your excitement?

3. What means of communication are available to inform residents of the service area about your new ministries? How can you most effectively invite them to participate?

Chapter 2 Tool

A Leadership Bible Study

The Old and New Testaments were written over a period of more than 1,000 years and tell stories of God's people that extend back even further. In those many centuries, God's people encountered many different situations and adopted a variety of leadership styles to meet the needs of each situation.

Read Judges 2:16-23.

In the time of the book of Judges, Israel was a very loose confederation of tribes. These tribes were linked by common heritage, language, cultural practices, and religious beliefs but had no central government. There were no taxes, but there also was no military in place for protection. Additionally, some other nearby tribes took advantage of Israel's lack of central authority by invading the nation.

It was in times of crisis that a judge arose to unite the tribes and lead them in a campaign of battle, or in some other way deal with the threat. Some ordinary individual, usually not someone with any special training or qualifications, and certainly without the benefit of an election, answered the call to lead.

After the immediate crisis had passed, the judge usually tried to pick up ordinary daily life as before. But the judge's new status as a national hero made ordinary life difficult. Because the judge had acquired a reputation among all the tribes as someone gifted by God to solve problems, it was only natural that individuals who had disputes with one another would seek out the judge as an arbiter, a role that often continued for many decades, either until the judge died, or until some other charismatic leader arose to meet a later challenge.

- How have times of crisis caused your community to organize itself differently?

- What qualifications do we expect from those who lead us in times of crisis?

- What expectations do we have of leaders after an immediate threat has passed?

Read 1 Samuel 8:4-9.

The last and, in many respects, the greatest of the judges was a priest named Samuel. Like some other judges, Samuel tried to retire from the limelight after each crisis, but again and again he was called back into service. At one point he even tried to delegate his judicial authority to his sons—a move that proved to be something of a disaster. It was after this failure that the people asked Samuel to appoint for them a king.

This request was very troubling for Samuel, because Israel had been founded upon the ideal that no human should be subject to another human, but that all should stand as equals under God's rule. Samuel warned the people of Israel that there would be a price to pay for the advantages of kingly leadership. Kings would need to levy taxes and conscript young people for military service. Once kings tasted power, they would become selfish, seizing land and wealth, and ultimately enslaving the people. Nevertheless, the people continued to insist on a king, and Samuel eventually agreed.

- How does the kingly style of leadership differ from that of a judge? What are the advantages and disadvantages of each style of leadership?

- Are there times in our own nation's history when we have been willing to give up some freedoms in exchange for the temporary advantages of strong leadership?

- Why was God willing to give the people what they asked for, even though God knew it would be harmful?

Read Numbers 18:20-24.

Aaron, the brother of Moses, became chief of the tribe of Levi. Because Aaron served as the first priest among the Israelites, the Levites became designated as the priestly tribe. Every male descendant of Aaron was automatically ordained a priest.

Not only was the priesthood a sacred trust for the Levites—it was essentially a family business. Lest they become diverted from their sacred charge, God decreed that the tribe of Levi should not inherit a portion of the promised land. They made their living solely from the offerings brought to the temple by faithful Israelites. In fact, people who were not Levites could not even enter the sacred areas of the temple, but stood back to watch the priests present their offerings to God on their behalf.

Today we usually expect the pastor of a congregation, except in special circumstances, to be devoted to ministry full time, and to be supported by the offerings of congregational members. The ministry is both a sacred trust and the profession by which that individual makes his or her living.

What are our expectations of pastors today?

- What are our expectations of pastors today? How are these expectations similar to or different from the expectations the people of Israel had of the Levites?

- Are there other people who consider the congregation to be their family concern or their inherited responsibility? In what ways is this communicated to others?

- For congregations today, what are the advantages of this type of leadership? What are the disadvantages?

Read Acts 2:41-47 and Acts 6:1-6.

The first of these readings describes a nearly ideal community of faith in which the apostles are functioning very much like Levite priests, making all of the decisions and doing all of the work. But just a few chapters later in the book of Acts, we read about the very first congregational disagreement. Because a style of leadership was not working well for the community, it was altered.

This new style of leadership has at least two distinct features. First, the clergy in this picture devote themselves entirely to preaching, teaching, visitation of the sick, and other pastoral tasks. All matters of policy concerning how the community will live, own property, distribute resources, and so forth are decided pastorally, based on doctrinal principles alone. Second, matters of administration, such as handling funds, making budgets, serving on various committees, and providing physical necessities for needy persons, are all picked up by the volunteer members of the community who were set apart for these duties.

- How does a congregation know when a style of leadership isn't working for them? If the model from Acts is followed, how should congregations go about changing that style?

- Is the division of labor described in these readings from Acts appropriate today? Should pastors be excluded from all administrative duties and decisions?

- It appears that there was a division between those disciples who spoke Hebrew as their first language, and the "Hellenists," whose first language was Greek. What kinds of divisions put a strain on congregational leadership today?

Read Revelation 2:1-7 and Revelation 3:1-6.

John, a bishop in Asia Minor, had been exiled to the island of Patmos by the Romans. From exile he wrote a single letter, which was to be passed among the seven congregations under his oversight as bishop. Because Roman soldiers read and censored his mail, John chose a style of writing called "apocalyptic." The apocalyptic writing style, with its strange visions and images, appeared to be nonsense to the Romans, so it was allowed to pass.

In each of the messages to the seven churches, the Risen Christ is described in slightly different terms. Then, each church is admonished for certain failings or encouraged as it faces particular problems, and most are praised for successes in faithfulness. Each church is addressed and evaluated in a unique way.

- As you compare these two passages, in what ways would you say these two congregations were different from one another?

- How do you think John of Patmos might have addressed your congregation if it were included among the churches to which he wrote?

- What are the advantages of being unique as a congregation? What are the disadvantages to not being the same as the church across the street or down the block?

What are the advantages of being unique as a congregation?

Congregational Model

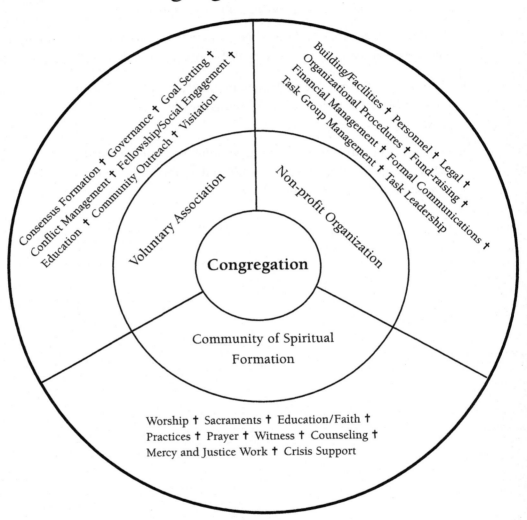

This illustration was adapted from "Model of Parish Leadership Functions" on page 80 of *The Management of Ministry*, by James D. Anderson and Ezra Earl Jones, ©1978 by James D. Anderson and Ezra Earl Jones. Reprinted by permission of Harper Collins Publishers, Inc.

Our Context: Exploring Our Congregation and Community, copyright © Augsburg Fortress. May be reproduced for local use.

Chapter 5 Tool

Defining Your Service Area

To begin, identify all zip codes where members of your congregation reside and calculate the percentage of your congregation's total membership residing in each. It would also be helpful to have available a map of zip code areas.

Primary service area

Enter only zip codes with at least 30% of current members residing there. (If the percentages for a zip code are so different from the others that averaging data across the zip codes would be misleading, move that zip code to the secondary service category.)

Zip code in which church is located: _____

Percentage of members: _____ %

Zip code with second largest percentage of members: _____

Percentage of members: _____ %

Zip code with third largest percentage of members: _____

Percentage of members: _____ %

If another zip code borders on one or more of the zip codes listed above and has grown more than 10% in population in recent years or is projected to increase the number of housing units significantly in the next five years, enter that zip code here as part of your primary service area:

_____

Your primary service area is made up of the one to four zip codes you have listed above. Show these zip code areas on a map. Identify the geographic boundaries of your primary service area, either by compass points from the church location or by landmarks such as highways. _____

What is the average travel time between the church building and the most distant part(s) of the primary service area? _____

Secondary service area

Not all congregations have a secondary service area. If the majority of new members who joined within the last five years live in a zip code not included in the primary service area, enter that zip code here: _____

If more than 10% but less than 30% of your members reside in another zip code, enter it here: _____

Note the maximum driving time estimated for the primary service area. If there is an area not adjacent to your primary service area but located only slightly beyond this travel time and showing significant growth in population (especially if new housing is being developed), enter that zip code here: _____

Chapter 5 Tool

Examining Your Service Area

1. Compile statistics for your congregation following the sample table below, or by using a spreadsheet created with your own software program. (You may not have 1990 or 2000 data if your congregation is fairly new.)
2. Create a separate table or spreadsheet for each of the following: your zip code, county, state, and the U.S. Compile statistics for each of these tables or spreadsheets, using information from the U.S. Census Bureau, ELCA or other denominational offices, government planning offices, local agencies, or market research firms. (If there is more than one zip code in your service area, combine the totals from each.)
3. Compare the results for your congregation with the information for your zip code, county, state, and the U.S.
4. Circle any statistics that indicate notable trends.

Note: Population is reported by total number. Median family income is reported by dollar amount. Remaining statistics are reported by percentages.

	1990	2000	This Year	In Five Years (projection)
Population				
Race and ethnicity* American Indian or Alaska Native Asian Black or African American Native Hawaiian or Other Pacific Islander White Hispanic or Latino Not Hispanic or Latino				
Age** 0-4 5-9 10-14 15-17 18-24 25-34 35-44 45-54 55-59 60-64 65-74 75 +				

Our Context: Exploring Our Congregation and Community, copyright © Augsburg Fortress. May be reproduced for local use.

	1990	2000	This Year	In Five Years (projection)
Median household income				
Educational attainment Less than Grade 9 Grade 9-12 (no diploma) High school grad or equivalency Some college (no degree) Associate degree Bachelor degree Graduate or professional degree				
Employment status Armed Forces Civilian employed Civilian unemployed Not in labor force				
Occupation Executive and managerial Professional specialty Technical support Sales Administrative support Private household service Protective service Other service Farming, forestry, and fishing Precision production, craft, and repair Machine operation, assembly, and inspection Transportation and material moving Labor				
Marital status Never married Married, spouse present Married, spouse absent, not separated Separated Widowed Divorced				
Types of households Married couple with children under 18 Married couple with no children under 18 Female householder with children under 18 Female householder with no children under 18 Male householder with children under 18 Male householder with no children under 18 Single or living with non-relatives Group quarters				

* The categories for race and ethnicity follow the minimum categories for race and ethnicity in the Office of Management and Budget's revised standards for federal data adopted in October 1997.

** Age statistics are grouped differently to achieve comparisons for different purposes. Two popular methods are to categorize age by life cycle stages (preschoolers, elementary school, and so on) or generations (or groups born during specific years, such as baby boomers).

Chapter 6 Tool

A Primer in Sampling

While it would be wonderful to speak with each resident of a congregation's service area, there usually isn't enough time and staff to talk to everyone. That's why professional researchers use a technique called sampling. This allows them to interview relatively few subjects but to project the results onto a much larger population with a small margin of error.

To try sampling, begin by determining the maximum number of households you are prepared to contact for the canvass. For example, if you have 12 volunteers ready to go in teams of two, and each of these 6 teams is willing to contact 8 households, you are prepared to contact 48 households (6 x 8 = 48).

Next, get a rough idea of how many households are in the area you wish to canvass. If your area is an entire city or town, the telephone directory makes a convenient list. Count the number of listings in just one column on one page of the directory, then multiply by the number of columns per page and the number of pages for your town. It isn't necessary to have the exact count, just a close estimate. If your service area does not have a single set of telephone listings, it may be possible to obtain a list of households from your local government. If no lists are readily available, you can arrive at a rough estimate simply by having the service area marked on a local map. Then, count the number of blocks in the area and multiply that number by the number of homes on a typical block. Once you have that estimate, you can divide the estimated number of households in the canvass area by the number of contacts you are prepared to make.

Carrying through on the example above, if you have enough volunteers for 48 visits, and if you arrived at an estimation of

Our Context: Exploring Our Congregation and Community, copyright © Augsburg Fortress. May be reproduced for local use.

1,050 households in your anticipated area, you would divide the number 1,050 by 48, and then come up with a result of approximately 21. This would mean that you would visit every 21st household, which might work out to about one home or apartment on each block.

**Prepare for
your visits
ahead of time.**

Finally, professional researchers sometimes note important distinctions within the area and adjust their sampling technique accordingly. For example, if the demographic data indicates that there are a large number of young, unmarried adults residing in apartments in the area, and that most single-family homes are inhabited by families or "empty nest" couples, it will be important that each segment of the population is represented in proportion. Make sure, in such a case, that the canvass includes apartment-dwellers and doesn't contact only people living in single family homes. Precise numbers are unimportant, but it is critical that the canvass includes a good mix of all of the types of people and households in the area.

Prepare for your visits ahead of time. Here are some things that can make it more likely that the welcome mat will be out for you:

- Let people know you're coming by sending a news release to the local newspaper, or placing an ad in the local advertising flyer. Announce that visitors from your congregation will knock on doors in the coming week, not to sell anything or to proselytize but simply to get feedback on how the congregation can better serve the community.

- If you are using a sampling technique that allows you to work from a list of households with addresses, send postcards in advance, again explaining the nature of the visits and politely requesting a few minutes of each recipient's time.

- Finally, don't be discouraged. Some doors will be closed in your face, but probably fewer than you suspect. When it happens, remember that many factors may lead neighbors to fear unknown visitors. Don't take this type of reaction personally.

Chapter 7 Tool

Creating Our Congregational Tapestry

Year	Events	Pastors/Leaders	Buildings	Important Changes

Gather a group of charter members (if possible), long-time members, and newer members. Working individually or in pairs, make a chart like the one above, leaving plenty of room to write. Fill in years, events, leaders, and other information as best as you can from memory. When you are done, gather in the large group to work out a complete "tapestry" of the life of your congregation.

• What threads or themes do you see woven in this story?

• What events or persons most affected the weave?

• What colors do you think this tapestry might display? Why?

• What is the overall look? If the weave has beauty, where does it come from?

• If it has knots and twists, where do they come from?

• If the tapestry had a title, what would the title be? Why?

Chapter 7 Tool

Inventory of Ministries

Sample

1. Create a chart similar to this sample. If you prefer, create a separate chart for each area of ministry (such as worship, learning, witness, service, and nurture and support).
2. List each ministry and its key leaders, frequency, time, place, participants, and any anticipated changes.

Ministry	Key Leaders	Frequency, Time, and Place	Participants	Anticipated Changes
Traditional Worship	Pastor Organist Choir Director Choirs	*Weekly* Sun. 9:00 a.m. Sanctuary	Open to all: Average attendance is 145	Teach Setting 5 from *With One Voice* this fall
"Prayer Chain" Group	J. Carter	*Weekly* Mon. 10:30 a.m. Church Library	14 women, all seniors	none
Chancel Choir	T. Cruz	*Weekly* Wed. 7:00 p.m. Sanctuary	18 adults	New robes to be purchased with a memorial gift

CPSIA information can be obtained
at www.ICGtesting.com
Printed in the USA
BVOW07s2002210717
489878BV00005B/42/P